BestMasters

Springer awards "BestMasters" to the best application-oriented master's theses, which were completed at renowned chairs of economic sciences in Germany, Austria, and Switzerland in 2013.
The works received highest marks and were recommended for publication by supervisors. As a rule, they show a high degree of application orientation and deal with current issues from different fields of economics.
The series addresses practitioners as well as scientists and offers guidance for early stage researchers.

Bernadette Gral

How Financial Slack Affects Corporate Performance

An Examination in an Uncertain and Resource Scarce Environment

With a foreword by Dr. Othmar Lehner

Springer Gabler

Bernadette Gral
Steyr, Austria

ISBN 978-3-658-04551-7
ISBN 978-3-658-04552-4 (eBook)
DOI 10.1007/978-3-658-04552-4

The Deutsche Nationalbibliothek lists this publication in the Deutsche Nationalbibliografie; detailed bibliographic data are available in the Internet at http://dnb.d-nb.de.

Library of Congress Control Number: 2013955626

Springer Gabler

Printed on acid-free paper

Springer Gabler is a brand of Springer DE.
Springer DE is part of Springer Science+Business Media.
www.springer-gabler.de

Geleitwort

Financial Slack, in der Form von finanziellem, ungenutztem Überschuss im Working Capital, wird in der Literatur stark kontrovers diskutiert. Lange Zeit, unter dem Dogma der Ressourceneffizienz, als Zeichen mangelhaften Managements angesehen, wird Financial Slack sukzessive in neuerer Literatur rehabilitiert und nunmehr als ein positiver Indikator für strategische Unternehmensentwicklung gewürdigt. Die Hintergründe dieser Dichotomie sind bis dato nicht geklärt, vermutet wird, dass eine bis dato nicht gefundene Moderator Variable zwischen den Zusammenhängen steht.

Die vorliegende Thesis untersucht in einem ersten Schritt aktuelle Literatur aus renommierten Journalen und fasst dabei Strömungen und Definitionen ausgezeichnet zusammen. Die dabei verwendete Literaturvielfalt und Qualität erfolgt dabei weitestgehend multidisziplinär. Eine durch die Autorin selbst erstellte Kategorisierung der gefundenen Literatur aus unterschiedlichen Perspektiven (transient vs. potential, easy- or hard to recover resources) zeigt starkes analytisches Geschick und legt die Grundlage für weitere empirische Forschung. Financial Slack wird in seinem Wesen diskutiert und Überlegungen zur Messbarkeit angestellt.

Im zweiten Teil nutzt die Autorin ein longitudinales quantitatives Studiendesign und untersucht Financial Slack am Beispiel von börsennotierten Pharmakonzernen während der Finanzkrise 2007 bis 2010. Dabei werden Hypothesen aus der Literatur abgeleitet und mittels geeigneter statistischer Methoden (deskriptiv sowie ANOVA und Regressionsanalyse) überprüft. Die Auswertung erfolgt methodisch robust und wird gut aufbereitet, sodass zahlreiche Erkenntnisse für Theorie und Praxis gewonnen werden können.

In der darauf folgenden Diskussion geht die Autorin ausführlich auf mögliche Störvariablen ein, untersucht u.a. die Auswirkung von M&A Aktivitäten sowie IPOs. Zur Absicherung führt die Autorin dann noch eine subsequente qualitative Dokumentenanalyse durch, um spezielle außergewöhnliche Vorkommnisse, die die Datenlage bei den einzelnen Unternehmen verfälschen könnten, zu identifizieren.

Financial Slack erweist sich als positiv im Sinne des Shareholder Values in Zeiten von unternehmerischen Transitionen wie M&A oder IPOs. Die Finanz- und Wirtschaftskrise führte bei den Unternehmen ebenfalls zu Transitionen aufgrund von strukturell notwendigen Anpassungsprozessen, sodass dieser Zeitraum höchst aufschlussreich für die Forschungsthematik erscheint.

Die Thesis trägt einen wesentlichen Baustein zu unserem Verständnis von Financial Slack bei. In ruhigen Fahrwassern ist Slack tatsächlich ein Zeichen ungenutzter Ressourcen – und damit von mangelnder Effizienz – während in Umbruchsphasen Slack als notwendiges Spielkapital für unternehmerische Veränderungen angesehen werden kann.

Dr. Othmar Lehner

Professor für Finanz- und Risikomanagement
FH Oberösterreich, Campus Steyr, Fakultät für Management

Dr. Othmar Lehner MBA is currently Director of Programme at the ACRN U. Centre for Research Methodology, Austria, Cambridge UK, and a full Professor of Finance and Risk Management at the University of Upper Austria. Previously he was a Lecturer in Entrepreneurship at the University of Jyväskylä, Finland. He studied Sociology, Business and Finance at the University of Linz, Austria and at the University of London.

After his Master in Finance, he went into a professional career working as a bank manager for 10 years before he continued his academic calling in a joint PhD programme of the University of Jyväskylä in Finland and Stanford University, California to complete one of the first Doctor of Science theses at that time in Social Entrepreneurship, under the examiners Johanna Mair from Stanford US and Kai Hockerts, CBS Denmark.

His research interests are Social Entrepreneurship, especially the comparative and political dimensions, Social Finance and Crowdfunding, in which he deals with issues of the interface between the public and social sectors; organizational legitimacy and governance; the development of social finance markets; and impact measurement and innovation. In 2011/12 he was a guest at Harvard U. in the research group assisting the Obama administration in creating the JOBS act. Dr Lehner is widely published in peer reviewed journals and is the author of the research book “Social Entrepreneurship Perspectives: Triangulated Approaches to Hybridity” at JSBE publishing house. He is a regular speaker at a range of international conferences and has held guest lectureships at a variety of academic institutions including: Oxford University SAID, Cambridge Hughes Hall, University of Heidelberg, University of Business and Economics Vienna. At the ACRN he leads a research consortium aiming to explore the dimensions of social and sustainable finance, and is responsible for the annual FRAP conference series of Finance, Risk and Accounting Perspectives. He also serves as associate editor at the Routledge Journal of Social Entrepreneurship and the Routledge Journal of Sustainable Finance and Investment.

Table of contents

Geleitwort V
Table of figures IX
List of tables XI
List of abbreviations XIII

1 Introduction 1

1.1 Problem definition 2

1.2 Goal of the thesis 3

1.3 Structure of the thesis 4

2 Methodology 5

2.1 Literature Review 5

2.2 Research design 6

2.3 Sample selection 8

2.4 Data collection 10

2.5 Measures 11

2.6 Data analysis 13

3 Literature review 17

3.1 Slack 17

3.1.1 Definition and conceptualization of slack 17

3.1.2 History of slack in literature 22

3.1.3 Role and functions of slack 25

3.1.4 Antecedents of slack 30

3.1.5 Measurement of slack 34

3.1.6 Potential utilization of slack 39

3.2 The relationship between slack and performance 45

3.2.1 Definition of performance 46

3.2.2 Theories and findings on the relationship ... 49
3.2.3 Intervening variables on the relationship ... 56
3.3 Uncertainty and munificence in the external environment ... 58
3.3.1 Definition of uncertainty and munificence ... 59
3.3.2 Impact of environmental uncertainty and munificence on slack ... 61
3.3.3 The financial crisis as an example for high uncertainty and low munificence ... 65
3.4 Summary ... 67
4 Propositions and hypotheses ... 69
4.1 Propositions and hypotheses concerning the impact of slack on performance ... 70
4.2 Propositions concerning intervening variables on the relationship ... 72
5 Empirical results ... 75
5.1 Quantitative correlational analysis ... 75
5.2 Qualitative content analysis ... 86
5.2.1 Novartis AG – most new products ... 87
5.2.2 Roche Holding AG – most M&A activities ... 91
5.2.3 Almirall SA – initial public offering ... 96
6 Discussion of the findings ... 99
7 Conclusion and forecast ... 105
7.1 Limitations of the study ... 106
7.2 Potential for future research ... 107
8 List of references ... 109

Table of figures

Figure 1: Research Procedure ... 5

Figure 2: Procedure of content analysis ... 15

Figure 3: Resource absorption / rarity matrix ... 21

Figure 4: Categories of Performance Measures ... 47

Figure 5: Pools of slack categories corresponding to the dimension of recoverability ... 53

Figure 6: Conceptual model ... 69

Figure 7: Scatterplot for regression analysis for the year 2010 ... 86

List of tables

Table 1: Sample firms 9

Table 2: Overview of financial indicators of slack 38

Table 3: Review of recent studies on the slack-performance link 52

Table 4: Correlations for the year 2007 77

Table 5: Descriptive statistics for the year 2007 78

Table 6: Correlations for the year 2008 79

Table 7: Descriptive statistics for the year 2008 80

Table 8: Correlations for the year 2009 81

Table 9: Descriptive statistics for the year 2009 82

Table 10: Correlations for the year 2010 83

Table 11: Descriptive statistics for the year 2010 84

Table 12: Regression analysis for the year 2010 85

List of abbreviations

approx.	approximately
cf.	lat.: confer, “compare“
EBIT	Earnings before interest and taxes
EBITDA	Earnings before interest, taxes, depreciation and amortization
EMA / EMEA	European Medicines Agency
e.g.	lat.: exempli gratia, “for example”
FDA	US Food and Drug Administration
GAAP	generally accepted accounting principles
HR	human resources
i.e.	lat.: id est, “that is”
IFRS	international financial reporting standards
IPO	initial public offering
M&A	mergers & acquisitions
NACE Rev. 2	statistical classification of economic activities in the European community, revision 2 (2008)
p.	page
pp.	pages
P/L	profit or loss
ROA	return on assets
ROA_{ni}	return on assets, using net income
$ROA_{pre\text{-}tax}$	return on assets, using profit or loss before tax
ROA_{EBITDA}	return on assets, using earnings before interest, taxes, depreciation and amortization
ROE	return on equity
ROI	return on investment

ROS	return on sales
UK	United Kingdom
US	United States of America
WTO	World Trade Organization

1 Introduction

An organization's resource management determines how competitive advantage and sustainable growth are achieved in a rapidly changing environment. Correspondingly the optimization of a firm's resource allocation patterns and the resulting impact on performance has substantive theoretical and practical implications (cf. Chiu and Liaw, 2009, p. 321). One of the main challenges in managing a company's resources is to constantly have the required level of resources available. On the one hand resource optimization is favorable in order to operate highly efficiently, while on the other hand having a buffer of resources ready to address unexpected threats and opportunities can be crucial. The implications of this dilemma are intensified during times of environmental change and external threat.

Organizational slack develops when a company holds resources which exceed the needed resources for its current operations. Bradley *et al.* (2011b, p. 537) describe the effect of slack as *„a double-edged sword, simultaneously fueling and hindering growth."* As indicated in this statement, in previous literature contradictory views on the role of organizational slack in the management of organizations exist.

A positive feature of organizational slack is that it acts as a buffer in rapidly changing environments and allows managers room for maneuver. Authors argue that slack can be used by companies to successfully adapt to external pressures, support innovations and experimentation, and make modifications to strategy as a response to changes in the environment. This perspective on slack is frequently maintained by resource based and behavioral theorists, who characterize slack as a valuable resource (cf. Lee, 2011, p. 4; Vanacker *et al.*, 2013, p. 6). This notion proposes that the presence of slack positively influences corporate performance, growth, innovation, market expansion, etc.

On the other hand, organizational slack can lead to waste in resource allocation. Researchers argue that when excess resources are available, managers acting as agents and become irrationally optimistic, inward looking, and risk averse. Hence, they tend to use excess resources for self-serving projects. Particularly organizational economists and agency theorists suggest this view of slack as inefficiency (cf. Lin *et al.*, 2009, p. 404; Su *et al.*, 2009, p. 77). In this context a negative effect of organizational slack on corporate performance, growth, and other organizational aspects is implied.

In an attempt to reconcile these opposing views, some researchers suggest that the relationship between slack and performance is curvilinear. Authors supporting this opinion assume that there is an optimal level of slack. They argue that slack positively affects organizational aspects such as innovation, performance, or growth within certain range, but inhibits those aspects beyond that range (cf. Chiu and Liaw, 2009, p. 335; Nohria and Gulati, 1997, p. 603). In other words, as long as firms have a cushion of resources large enough to address unexpected threats and opportunities, but small enough to avoid managers' irresponsible behavior, slack benefits a firm. Additionally the external environment strongly influences slack and its effect on performance (cf. Bradley *et al.*, 2011a, p. 1072).

Although previous studies provide numerous useful insights, there is still a need for further theorizing and empirical study on the effect of organizational slack within a firm. The research gaps are discussed in the problem definition.

1.1 Problem definition

Prior literature and empirical investigation on organizational slack show certain inconsistencies and offer room for further research. Studies on the effect of financial slack on performance indicate that the empirical results are not generalizable for varying environments. In order to understand the relationship of slack and performance it is crucial to pay particular attention to the environmental context (cf. Latham and Braun, 2009, pp. 33–34). Specifically, high uncertainty, complexity or threat in the environment, as well as scarcity of resources and opportunities are highlighted as essential influencing factors by previous authors (cf. Bradley *et al.*, 2011a, p. 1074). The global financial crisis that started in 2007, serves as a recent example for rapid environmental change, implicating increased external uncertainty and resource scarcity. It posed a significant environmental threat to firms' survival and profitability, and thus offers a unique possibility to study slack in the context of external threat.

Furthermore, a closer investigation of factors that condition or moderate the relationship of slack and performance is required due to partially conflicting results of prior work. Additionally, it is essential to control for industry effects when examining the influence of slack (cf. Daniel *et al.*, 2004, p. 572; Wefald *et al.*, 2010b, p. 71).

Finally, partially contradictory and coinciding categories for organizational slack exist (cf. Krcal, 2012, pp. 683–685. Different slack types (e.g. available, recoverable and potential slack), which interact differently with performance measures, are investigated in prior studies (cf. Sigerstad, 2004, p. 44). Furthermore used samples and measurement of variables differ widely among studies (cf. Daniel *et al.*, 2004, p. 565). In addition methodological issues exist among previous studies. While some authors apply one measure others use multiple measures for slack and / or performance (cf. Greenley and Oktemgil, 1998, p. 378).

1.2 Goal of the thesis

This thesis addresses the above mentioned gaps in the literature by revisiting the relationship between financial slack and corporate performance. Specifically the author examines whether financial slack influences the performance of European pharmaceutical companies during times of crisis. Thereby this paper makes several contributions to the literature on the slack-performance relationship.

First, in this paper several intervening variables are suggested and their influence on slack and / or performance is examined. Specifically, innovative capacity (number of new product approvals), M&A activities and IPO events are studied as moderators on the slack-performance link. To account for the need to control for industry effects, this study selects a sample of European pharmaceutical firms. The pharmaceutical industry is a very research intensive sector (cf. European Commission, 2011, p. 6). Therefore organizational slack and its effects on innovation, risk taking and performance play a crucial role.

Besides, this thesis answers the call of previous authors to study the relation between slack and performance in the face of a threatening external environment (cf. Bradley *et al.*, 2011a, p. 1074; Latham and Braun, 2009, p. 34). The global financial crisis between 2007 and 2010 presents significant environmental threats to organizations survival and profitability, and thus was chosen as the context to investigate the slack-performance relationship.

In order to shed some light on the inconsistencies concerning the theory of slack, the literature review further deals with the conceptualization of organizational slack and its functions as well as the measurement of different forms of slack.

1.3 Structure of the thesis

The remainder of this thesis is in the following format. In a first step the methodology, research design as well as the used measures for empirical investigation are explained. Thereafter, a review of existing literature is presented, where the concept of organizational slack, its antecedents and functions as well as measurement and potential utilization are discussed. Additionally previous findings concerning slack and its effects, as well as the external environment as an influencing factor are considered.

Creating research questions out of the debated theory, propositions and null hypotheses are formulated. In the empirical part of this thesis the author tests the hypotheses through correlational and regression analysis. Subsequently, the results of the quantitative analysis are discussed and more in depth qualitative research on salient results is performed. Finally, the author compares the results of the empirical analysis with existing findings from the literature and offers suggestions for further research.

2 Methodology

In this section the author describes the research approach adopted in this thesis. First, the characteristics of the literature review are explained. Thereafter, the research design, methodology and sample selection is argued. Additionally, the processes of data collection and analysis are discussed. The research procedure includes several sequential steps as shown in detail in Figure 1. However, the explanation of the methodology in this chapter is arranged logically and does not follow the exact steps of the actual research procedure.

2.1 Literature Review

The aim of the study of literature is to compare and summarize the findings of existing work concerning slack, its influence on performance as well as the impact of the external environment on the relationship. Therefore the current state of literature and existing theories and concepts on the topic are analyzed. The findings and problems identified in previous research form the basis for further empirical investigation.

The focus of the literature review lies on articles published in academic journals and magazines, as well as specialized books. While German language results are included, English-language academic articles are emphasized.

The databases used for the literature research are:

- EBSCO Business Source Premier,
- Science Direct College Edition,
- Wiley Online Library,
- ABI/Inform Global Pro Quest, and
- JSTOR.

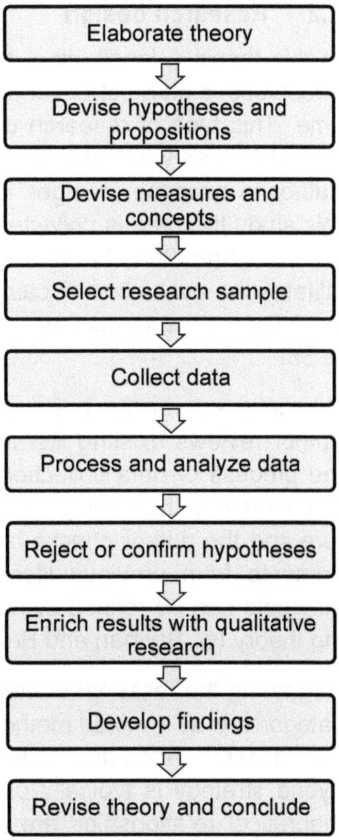

Figure 1: Research Procedure adapted from Bryman and Bell (2011, p. 151)

In addition, a search for supplementary material is performed on scholar.google.com. The keywords primarily used are organizational slack, financial slack, performance, crisis, munificence, and uncertainty. Besides, the author searched for slack in combination with innovation, risk, growth, acquisitions, intervening variables, IPO, M&A, antecedents, measurement, external environment, crisis, threat and economic downturn.

Specific propositions are devised on the basis of the literature review and null hypotheses are formulated. All further steps in the research process are explained in the following sections.

2.2 Research design

In this thesis a longitudinal research design is adopted. Hence, repeated observations on a set of variables for the same sample units are made over time. This type of research design is frequently used to discover relationships between variables. In contrast to a cross sectional design it allows the author to examine changes over a specific period of time. Specifically, in this study the data is collected for several years as the period of investigation runs from 2007 to 2010. An essential benefit of this design is that it facilitates the evaluation of causality between variables since the direction of the influence becomes more apparent over time (cf. Bryman and Bell, 2011, p. 58).

Primarily, a deductive approach to link theory and research is adopted. The author reviews existing literature and deduces hypotheses. Consequently, the process of data collection is based on and guided by existing theory. Subsequently the findings from the research are compared with the literature and the author checks how well the results support the theoretical arguments from previous literature. Through inductive reasoning, existing concepts can be refined or refuted and the findings contribute to the existing theory (cf. Bryman and Bell, 2011, p. 11).

Regarding the research strategy, the approach applied in this thesis can be categorized as a mixed method approach combing quantitative and qualitative research. According to Edmondson and McManus (2007, p. 1165) this hybrid strategy is typically used in intermediate theory, where provisional theoretical relationships are proposed or an established theory is transferred to a new context. As will be discussed in the literature review of the present thesis, the concept of slack is well established in literature, and can therefore be categorized as mature literature. Also the slack-performance relationship has been studied repeatedly, however partly inconsistent result are reported. Particularly the context of environmental threat has first recently become the focus of various studies. Consequently the author categorizes the relevant theory for the answer of the research question of this study as intermediate.

Overall, when applying a mixed method approach, it is essential that quantitative and qualitative research findings are integrated or linked in order to extract the maximum benefits of the study (cf. Bryman and Bell, 2011, p. 693). Regarding this thesis, the advantage of the hybrid method is that it enables the author to supplement quantitative results on the relationship between certain variables with fuller explanations based on qualitative data (cf. Edmondson and McManus, 2007, p. 1166).

Creswell (2003, p. 211), and Bryman and Bell (2011, p. 632) note several factors that are of importance when selecting a mixed method approach. First, the priority of qualitative or quantitative data and analysis plays an important role. The quantitative research approach is dominant in this thesis, since the main research question is answered through quantitative testing. Qualitative data is subsequently used to give a more detailed insight on a few salient results. Second, the implementation sequence of data collection of qualitative and quantitative data has to be determined. In this thesis the implementation is in phases, as quantitative data is collected first, and qualitative data is collected subsequently.[1] Creswell (2003, p. 211) adds that the stage in the process of the project for integration of the findings from the qualitative and quantitative perspective has to be determined. Since the data collection and analysis are performed individually, the integration of the findings is first conducted in the interpretation phase of this study.

According to Creswell (2003, p. 218) the approach applied in this thesis can be categorized as a sequential explanatory research strategy. Qualitative results are used to provide important contextual information as a supplement to quantitative findings. Thereby the qualitative research supports the explanation and interpretation of the findings on the intervening variables identified in quantitative research (cf. Bryman and Bell, 2011, pp. 636–639).

---

[1] More precisely, data collection for the independent and dependent variables is conducted first. Data collection for intervening variables and qualitative analysis is conducted simultaneously but analyzed individually. The process will be explained in detail in chapter 2.4 Data collection.

Specifically, in this thesis salient results of the quantitative research will be analyzed and enriched by qualitative research.

Further details on the method of data analysis, including the quantitative research (correlational analysis) and the qualitative research (content analysis) are explained in the section "Data analysis".

2.3 Sample selection

The author of this study uses financial data from a sample of publicly traded pharmaceutical firms to determine how financial slack affects performance. Specifically, companies operating in the pharmaceutical industry classified as NACE Rev. 2 primary code 212 (manufacture of pharmaceutical preparations) are chosen. In addition, the sample is limited to the region of Eastern and Western Europe, resulting in an initial sample of 9,697 firms.

The pharmaceutical industry is selected as a research context, for several reasons. While various different industries have been examined previously, the author of this thesis did identify any studies concerning slack and performance that focus on the pharmaceutical industry. Besides, in the years under investigation pharmaceutical companies accumulated high cash holdings (cf. 2008). For instance, Bloomberg reports that the world's biggest pharmaceutical companies were holding about $100 billion in cash and marketable securities in 2009 (cf. Kelley, 2009). Since cash holdings are an essential indicator for the presence of financial slack (cf. Bradley *et al.*, 2011a, p. 1081), the pharmaceutical industry seems to be a fitting research context for studying the effect of financial slack on performance. In addition, this industry is one of the most research intensive sectors in the European Union (cf. European Commission, 2011, p. 6). Therefore organizational slack plays a crucial role as it effects innovation, risk taking, acquisition activities and performance.

From the group of pharmaceutical firms located in Europe, those that provide consolidated financial statement for the period of 2007 to 2010 are selected (236 firms). In order to exclude subsidiaries and other affiliates, the parent companies (group ultimate owner or firms with named individuals or families as ultimate owners) are identified. Furthermore only firms, which provide the necessary data for the variables used in the empirical model for all the years between 2007 and 2010, are selected. Finally, from the remaining group of 110 firms the ones with the highest operating revenue (turnover) are chosen, resulting in a final sample of 25 firms.

	Company name	Ctry	Operating rev. in th EUR 2010	No. of employees 2010	Indepen-dency	Legal form	BvD ID number
1.	Actelion LTD	CH	1,534,967	2,441	A+	Public	CH28030030288
2.	Akzo Nobel NV	NL	14,697,000	55,590	A+	Public	NL09007809
3.	Almirall SA	ES	1,002,088	3,012	B+	Public	ESA58869389
4.	AstraZeneca PLC	GB	25,505,303	61,100	A+	Public	GB02723534
5.	Bayer AG	DE	35,704,000	111,400	A+	Public	DE5330000056
6.	Biomerieux SA	FR	1,379,700	6,365	D	Public	FR673620399
7.	Farmacol SA	PL	1,293,083	n.a.	B+	Public	PL273352747
8.	Galenica AG	CH	2,740,460	5,535	B+	Public	CH03530017094
9.	GlaxoSmithKline PLC	GB	33,602,640	98,485	A+	Public	GB03888792
10.	Krka DD Novo Mesto	SI	1,021,909	8,569	A+	Public	SI5043611
11.	Meda AB	SE	1,337,705	2,593	A+	Private	SE5564272812
12.	Merck KGAA	DE	9,363,900	40,562	C	Public	DE6050108507
13.	Novartis AG	CH	39,490,659	119,418	A+	Public	CH27030020612
14.	Novo Nordisk A/S	DK	8,186,689	30,014	B+	Public	DK24256790
15.	Paul Hartmann AG	DE	1,660,304	9,982	B+	Public	DE7370021237
16.	Pelion SA	PL	1,467,543	7,208	A+	Public	PL470929074
17.	Protek OAO	RU	2,453,985	12,370	B+	Public	RU59149045
18.	Richter Gedeon RT	HU	997,871	10,176	B+	Private	HU10484878
19.	Roche Holding AG	CH	39,124,377	80,653	B+	Public	CH27030051590
20.	Sanofi	FR	32,394,000	101,575	A+	Public	FR395030844
21.	Shire PLC	GB	2,597,804	4,183	A+	Public	GB30837EX
22.	Solvay SA	BE	5,993,000	16,785	B+	Private	BE0403091220
23.	Stada Arzneimittel AG	DE	1,657,343	8,024	A+	Public	DE6290015517
24.	Ucb NV/SA	BE	3,218,000	8,898	B+	Private	BE0403053608
25.	Warner Chilcott PLC	IE	2,224,912	2,700	A+	Public	IE471506

Table 1: Sample firms

It is important to mention that for a large number of European firms, especially for small or not publicly listed firms, no consolidated balance sheets or no financial data at all are available. Additionally due to the criterion "high operating revenue" only large firms are included in the sample. The author is aware of the limitation of the sample coverage in terms of firm size, which may cause selection bias. Besides, due to the small sample size of the study, the results cannot simply be generalized.

2.4 Data collection

The data collection in this thesis is based on secondary data. While primary data is often seen as subordinate to secondary data, secondary analysis can have substantial advantages. One major field of application for secondary data is, when historical information is of interest. Specifically, the problems of recall are resolved when past events are investigated through secondary data which has been created during the relevant time period (cf. Harris, 2001, p. 193). The use of archival material delivers large quantities of inexpensive data, and in addition is an unobtrusive strategy as archival material is nonreactive to the presence of investigators (cf. Berg, 2001, p. 191). Since the financial crisis of 2007 to 2010 is in the focus of this study, the benefits of unobtrusive secondary analysis can be exploited in this thesis. However, it has to be noted that due to the use of secondary data the researcher has no control over the quality of the data (cf. Bryman and Bell, 2011, p. 321).

The indicators for financial slack and performance are devised from publicly available data on balance sheets as well as profit and loss statements. The source of the financial data is the OSIRIS database offered by Bureau Van Dijk, which contains financial information on globally listed public companies.

The information about M&A and IPO deals is taken from Zephyr database, also offered by Bureau Van Dijk. Specifically, new acquisitions, acquisitions of increased stakes and the formation of joint ventures which were completed within the years 2007 to 2010 were included as M&A activities. The number of new product introductions, as an intervening variable is identified through an examination of mass media outputs. In addition, for the firm with most M&A activities, as well as for one firm undergoing an IPO, a newspaper research is conducted. The newspaper research for the qualitative as well as quantitative analysis includes the daily newspapers Financial Times (including FT.com) and The Wall Street Journal, as well as news from the international news agency Reuters Newswires. Particularly, articles published between 2007 and 2010 are in the focus. The newspaper research resulted in 2,693 articles for the quantitative correlational research as well as 1,099 articles for the supplementary qualitative research. To identify and organize the relevant data from the articles, a content analysis is conducted as described in the section "Data analysis".

2.5 Measures

For the quantitative analysis measures to operationalize the concepts of financial slack and performance, as well as the three intervening variables are defined in this section.

The *independent variable* in this analysis is financial slack, measured as the current ratio of a firm at the year end. The current ratio is a continuous interval variable and is calculated as follows:

$$\text{current ratio} = \frac{\text{current assets}}{\text{current liabilities}}$$

Current ratio has been chosen, because this measure was widely adopted as a measure of financial, available of unabsorbed slack by previous authors (cf. Daniel *et al.*, 2004). Since this ratio measures a firm's ability to pay its short term obligations it captures the unabsorbed nature of available financial slack.

The *dependent variable* in this study is corporate performance. The author uses an accounting based profitability measure for performance, namely return on assets (ROA) at the year end. This measure can also be categorized as a continuous interval ratio. Various definitions for the measure ROA exist in literature. Although several studies emphasize that ROA is widely used to measure performance in slack literature (cf. Lee, 2011, p. 10; Chiu and Liaw, 2009, p. 328), authors apply different definitions of the metric. The textbook definition of ROA is net income divided by total assets (cf. Losbichler *et al.*, 2012, p. 125). Besides, profit before tax can be used in order to cancel out any taxation differences as well as extraordinary P/L. Others focus on operating profit before interest, taxes, depreciation and amortization, thereby excluding e.g. differences in the capital structure of firms (e.g. Love and Nohria, 2005; Ju and Zhao, 2009). Each of these definitions has its advantages. In this study, three different, but commonly used definitions of ROA are applied in order to demonstrate the implications of differing definitions.

$$ROA_{ni} = \frac{\text{Net Income}}{\text{Total Assets}}$$

$$ROA_{pre\text{-}tax} = \frac{\text{P/L before tax}}{\text{Total Assets}}$$

$$ROA_{EBITDA} = \frac{\text{EBITDA*}}{\text{Total Assets}}$$

* EBITDA = Earnings before interest, taxes, depreciation and amortization

Some authors argue that a common problem of using ROA as a performance measure is that it varies strongly across industries (cf. Carton and Hofer, 2007, p. 85). This issue is overcome by the focus on a single industry in this study. Furthermore, several previous researchers argue that it is appropriate to consider a time lag when investigating the effect of performance on slack (cf. Su *et al.*, 2009, p. 81). Since especially absorbed forms of slack first have to be recovered it may take a considerable amount of time before slack shows its impact on performance. In this study no time lag is included in the analysis, because available slack is rather readily employable. The fact that a time lag does not have a significant effect on the strength of the relationship between any form of slack and performance is confirmed by Daniel *et al.* (2004, p. 572).

In addition to the two measures described, *three intervening variables* are considered in this study, namely M&A, new products and IPO. The number of M&A deals conducted during the investigation period is used as a measure for expansion. The number of new products introduced is used as a measure for the innovation activities of a firm. In this regard it has to be noted that only products that gained official approval during the sample period were counted. Other innovation activities or products in development which lack formal approval or have been rejected by the U.S. Food and Drug Administration (FDA) or European Medicines Agency (EMEA or EMA[2]) are not included in the analysis. Finally the undergoing of IPOs is

[2] From 1995 to 2004, the European Medicines Agency was known as European Agency for the Evaluation of Medicinal Products, short EMEA (cf. European Medicines Agency, 2009). Since the official launch of a new organizational structure and visual identity in November 2009 the acronym EMA has been commonly used.

included as a measure. All three variables are defined as the number of activities carried out per year, thus they are discrete. However, since the relatively large number of categories they generate, the intervening variables are treated as interval ratios and included in the Pearson's r correlational analysis. Specifically, they are regarded as moderating variables on the relationship between slack and performance. Thus they are expected to correlate with slack and /or performance and have a strengthening effect on the slack-performance relationship.

2.6 Data analysis

As mentioned above, in the first step of analysis the effect of financial slack on performance is investigated through correlational research. Intervening variables, identified through quantitative content analysis, are included in the correlational research. Subsequently three sample firms with salient results concerning the moderators are chosen and further qualitative content analysis of the data is performed.

The *correlational analysis* is concerned with the investigation of the relationship between financial slack and performance. Specifically, the analysis focuses on the question, if an influence of slack on performance is present in the pharmaceutical industry and which intervening variables exist. Descriptive statistics for the collected data for each variable, particularly results from the univariate analysis such as measures of central tendency and measures of dispersion are presented. In order to reject or confirm the null hypotheses a bivariate analysis of the variables for financial slack and performance, as well as the intervening variables is conducted in pairs. For that matter Pearson's product-moment correlation coefficients (Pearson's r) are calculated on a year by year basis (cf. Rasch, 2010, pp. 15–21; Bryman and Bell, 2011, pp. 344–349). In addition to the calculation of correlations, a test for statistical significance is performed. This allows the author to assess if the results of the analysis are generalizable to the population (cf. Bryman and Bell, 2011, p. 353). Subsequently, the author prepares a linear regression analysis for the year 2010 to further analyze the relationship between the independent and dependent variable.

The three intervening variables M&A, new products and IPO are included in the analysis in order to examine their moderating effect on the strength of the relationship. The method of *content analysis* is used in this regard to quantify the content of the articles identified in the newspaper research objectively and systematically (cf. Bryman and Bell, 2011, p. 291). The results of the newspaper research are additionally used in the second step of this thesis, the supplementary qualitative research, in order to enrich the quantitative findings from the correlational research. In this regard, three firms are chosen from the sample and qualitative content analysis is performed on the respective newspaper articles.

It is difficult to give a general definition of content analysis, since the interpretation of the term largely depends on the specific research field and purpose (cf. Mayring, 2010, p. 11). The author of this thesis understands content analysis as to the examination of documents and texts in an attempt to objectively and systematically analyze their content (cf. Harris, 2001, p. 103). This research approach lies at the intersection between qualitative and quantitative research (cf. Duriau *et al.*, 2007, p. 5). One of the main advantages of a content analysis approach is that it is an objective and transparent method, guided by specific rules. Thus the results can be replicated rather easily, and validity and reliability of data collection can be demonstrated (cf. Harris, 2001, p. 193). Besides, it is an unobtrusive and nonreactive research method since previously recorded data is analyzed. This makes it also appropriate for longitudinal analysis. In addition, content analysis provides a high level of flexibility (cf. Bryman and Bell, 2011, p. 305). By using this approach for both, thorough quantitative analysis as well as rich qualitative insight, the author exploits the advantages of content analysis to support the hybrid research strategy (cf. Duriau *et al.*, 2007, p. 23).

Quantitative content analysis emphasizes the identification and quantification of specific characteristics of the content e.g. the counting of textual elements to retrieve data. Qualitative content analysis on the other hand seeks to understand aspects such as the conditions and consequences of the factors under investigation and deals with the meaning in the specific context (cf. Berg, 2001, pp. 241–242; Bryman and Bell, 2011, pp. 289–291). Nevertheless qualitative context analysis demands a systematic, well-structured and controlled analysis, following explicit rules of coding and step by step models (cf. Mayring, 2010, pp. 48–49).

Consequently both, the quantitative and qualitative content analysis follow similar steps, as shown in Figure 2.

Since the results of content analysis depend strongly on the quality of the materials used for analysis (cf. Bryman and Bell, 2011, p. 308), the sources have to be chosen carefully. As mentioned before the material to be examined in this study is newspaper articles from the daily newspapers Financial

Times (including FT.com) and The Wall Street Journal, as well as news from the international news agency Reuters Newswires between 2007 and 2010. These sources are selected since they provide substantial coverage of international business and commercial news in Europa and the US, and are available to the author in the searchable press database Factiva. Concerning new products all articles related to new patents, new products and new product approvals are investigated. For M&A activities and IPO the search concentrates on articles related to acquisitions, mergers or takeovers and IPO deals respectively.

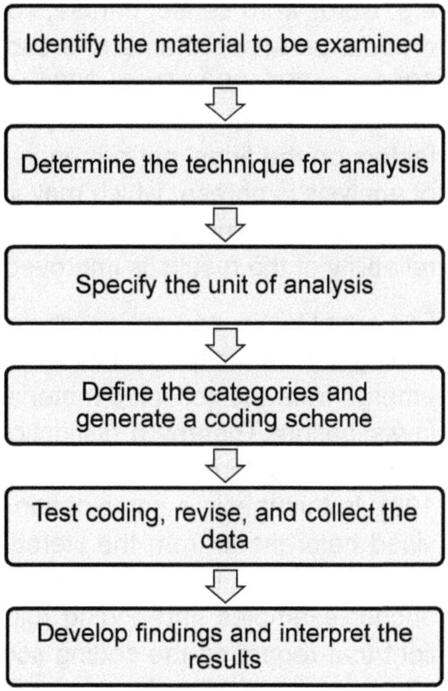

Figure 2: Procedure of content analysis adapted from Harris, 2001, p. 194 and Mayring, 2010, p. 60

The second step of the procedure is specifically important in qualitative content analysis. Generally three basic techniques for qualitative content analysis exist, namely summarizing, explication, and content-based structuring. Summarizing is performed to reduce the material up to its main content, resulting in a short text reflecting the key information. The goal of explication is to collect further material on the context of certain passages in order to improve the interpretation and understanding of the material. Content-based structuring refers to classifying and arranging the material according to pre-defined dimensions and categories (cf. Mayring, 2010, p. 65). For the qualitative part of this thesis a combination of structuring and summarizing is used. First structuring allows identifying and organizing the relevant articles and elements of data within them. Subsequently the data is summarized, focusing on the main content relevant to the research questions. Regarding the quantitative content analysis the author identifies the number of activities that occurred for each firm in the sample period, e.g. the number of approved products.

The unit of analysis is the basic unit of text to be counted and classified. The unit of analysis as well as the categories should be consistent with the nature of the research question (cf. Berg, 2001, p. 248). Common units are e.g. word, word sense, phrase, sentence or paragraph, as well as actor (individual persons), theme and subject, or disposition (cf. Bryman and Bell, 2011, pp. 295–298); Berg, 2001, p. 244). In this study the research question related to the qualitative analysis includes the identification of influencing factors on the firms' performance in the newspaper articles. Hence, the unit of analysis is phrase, which may vary from a single word to a sentence. The advantage of hand coding phrases, as implemented in this study, is that the reliability of the results is improved (cf. Harris, 2001, p. 199).

For quantitative as well as qualitative content analysis the categories for coding are formally established before the actual analysis of data. They emerge from the collected material and the existing literature on topic under investigation. Thereby a distinction can be made between the inductive or deductively determined categories (cf. Berg, 2001, p. 245; Harris, 2001, p. 199). In this thesis a combination of both is used. Thus, categories are devised beforehand from the literature and supplemented by categories that come up during the data analysis. For each category a distinct definition, anchor examples and coding rules are determined. Several authors highlight that regarding the coding scheme the defined dimension must be discrete (separate) in order to avoid conceptual or empirical overlap, and the categories must be mutually exclusive and sufficiently exhaustive in order to account for each variation of message. The development of such a coding scheme creates increased objectivity, transparency and minimizes the intrusion of bias (cf. Berg, 2001, pp. 240–241; Bryman and Bell, 2011, pp. 300–303).

After the categories and coding guidelines are defined, first testing of the coding scheme on a small portion of the articles is conducted. This includes the coding of 50 articles and the entry of the data into an excel spreadsheet. Subsequently the coding scheme is revised and some coding rules are modified. Finally all articles (1,099 articles for the qualitative analysis and 2,693 articles for the quantitative analysis) are coded in accordance with the coding schemes and the collected data is entered into excel spreadsheets. Based on the data the author develops findings and interprets the results of the content analysis. In this thesis, the quantitative content analysis is used to identify the number of new product approvals of firms for the correlational research. The findings from the qualitative content analysis are used to enrich the results of the correlational analysis and to give a deeper insight in the effect of the intervening variables.

3 Literature review

In the review of literature the theories concerning organizational slack and its effect on various organizational aspects are debated. The literature review is structured as follows. First the concept of organizational slack is discussed in detail. In this regard, definitions of organizational slack from prior literature and commonly used categorizations are described. In addition, the role of slack as well as its antecedents, measurement and possible utilization are explained. In the next section the author addresses the effect of slack on performance. In this context, potentially intervening variables on the relationship of the two factors are identified from existing literature. Finally, in the last section of the literature review the relationship of slack and performance is discussed in the context of external threat. Specifically, the recent financial crisis is brought up as an example of high external uncertainty and scarcity of financial resources.

3.1 Slack

3.1.1 Definition and conceptualization of slack

Over time the definition of organizational slack has been well established in literature (cf. Daniel *et al.*, 2004, p. 566). Nevertheless authors use various characteristics, functions or states of slack to describe and categorize the term. In the following section commonly used definitions and categorizations of slack are specified.

The work of James March in the late 1950s and early 1960s constitutes the basis for the first definition of organizational slack in literature (cf. Bourgeois, 1981, p. 30). In one of his first attempts to define the term slack, he described it as *"the difference between total resources and total necessary payments."* (Cyert and March, 1963, p. 42)

Referring to the literature of March, Bourgeois (1981, p. 30) defines organizational slack as a *"cushion of actual or potential resources which allows an organization to adapt successfully to internal pressures for adjustment or to external pressures for change in policy, as well as to initiate changes in strategy with respect to the external environment."* This definition is commonly used in management literature and frequently cited recent papers focusing on organizational slack and its functions and effects (cf. Mousa, 2009, p. 25).

More recent definitions of slack, which differ slightly from the original ones, can be found e.g. in the following papers:

(1) Nohria and Gulati (1996, p. 1246) define slack as *"the pool of resources in an organization that is in excess of the minimum necessary to produce a given level of organizational output."*

(2) Mishina *et al.* (2004, p. 1182) state that *"Slack is a dynamic quantity that represents the difference between the resources currently possessed by a firm and the resource demands of the current business."*

(3) George (2005, p. 661) notes that *"Slack is potentially utilizable resources that can be diverted or redeployed for the achievement of organizational goals."*

Krcal (2012, pp. 683–685) criticizes that the definitions and categorizations of slack in literature differentiate insufficiently between functions, states and types of slack. As a result, existing categories of slack are partially contradictory or coinciding. He argues that it is crucial to distinguish between types, functions, states and antecedents of slack in order to provide logical and consistent framework.

To give an overview of the types of slack categorized in literature, six different classifications of slack are presented in the following section of this thesis:

(1) Level of availability: available, recoverable and potential slack

(2) Level of absorption: unabsorbed and absorbed slack

(3) Level of deployment: generated and invested slack

(4) Level of discretion: high discretion and low discretion slack

(5) Resource availability / Resource demand: transient slack

(6) Type of resource (financial, operational, human resource, etc.)

The most commonly used categorizations of slack in recent literature originate from the papers of Bourgeois, Singh, and Sharfman written in the 1980s (cf. Krcal, 2012, p. 681).

(1) Level of availability: available, recoverable and potential slack

Bourgeois III and Singh (1983, p. 43) describe three states of slack along the dimension of availability, namely available, recoverable and potential slack. For (1) available slack they give the example of excess liquidity, since this type of resource is not yet integrated into the organization's system. (2) Recoverable slack on the other hand is already committed to specific organizational functions as excess costs (e.g. excess overhead costs), but there is the option of recovery in the future. Finally, (3) potential slack consists of potential future resources that can be generated by the organization from the environment, e.g. additional debt or equity capital (cf. Bourgeois III and Singh, 1983, p. 43).

(2) Level of absorption: unabsorbed and absorbed slack

Later, Singh (1986, p. 567) advances and refines this concept of categorization by adding the level of absorption of slack. He distinguishes between (1) unabsorbed slack, which *"corresponds to excess, uncommitted liquid resources in organizations"* and (2) absorbed slack, which *"corresponds to excess costs in organizations"* (Singh, 1986, p. 567).

Heng and Wefald add to Singh's definition that the two categories of slack differ significantly in their accessibility. Since unabsorbed slack is currently uncommitted it can be used easily and immediately, thus involving a higher level of flexibility. Absorbed slack on the other hand is already committed to a specific use and embedded in the company's system (e.g. in salaries, overhead expense and other administrative costs), which is why it is more difficult to be redeployed (cf. Heng and Xiuhao, 2010, p. 2; Wefald *et al.*, 2010b, p. 73). This distinction shows several similarities with the categories of availability, suggested by Bourgeois III and Singh (1983, p. 43).

(3) Level of deployment: generated and invested slack

Greenley and Oktemgil (1998) citing Chakravarthy (1986) use the level of deployment to distinguish between generated and invested slack. They define generated slack as available resources for the development of strategic options and the improvement of flexibility. This includes the ability to generate liquid resources and raise additional debt or equity. Invested slack consists of deployed resources, which may reduce the opportunity to develop strategic options and inhibit flexibility (e.g. slack invested in salaries, working capital, assets, etc.). Again, this classification is similar to the characterization of slack along the dimensions of availability or absorption.

(4) Level of discretion: high discretion and low discretion slack

Taking the previously developed categories of Bourgeois and Singh into account, Sharfman *et al.* (1988, p. 602) suggest the classification of slack by level of managerial discretion. He describes two different forms of slack, namely high and low discretion slack. (1) High discretion slack can be deployed very flexibly and consists of e.g. cash, cash equivalents, credit lines, raw materials inventory, low skilled labor, and highly flexible machine capacity. (2) Low discretion slack on the other hand, can only be used in more specific situations and includes e.g. processed inventory, skilled labor and low flexibility machine capacity.

(5) Resource availability / Resource demand: transient slack

Later, George (2005, p. 664) introduces yet another categorization of slack, namely transient slack. This type of slack refers to excess resources available after resource demands have been met and emphasizes the ephemerality and dynamic nature of slack resources. Transient slack represents the difference between resource availability and resource demand. The author highlights that even though firms possess the same amount of resources, the current resource needs for their business might differ, resulting in differing levels of transient slack.

(6) Type of resource: financial, operational, human resource, etc.

In addition to Singh's (1986, p. 567) classification of slack by level of absorption, Voss *et al.* (2008, p. 149) use the level of rarity to describe four different forms of slack. Regarding the level or rarity they draw a distinction between generic resources and rare resources. Where (1) generic resources are commonly available and relatively easy to acquire (e.g. liquid assets, production capacity), and (2) rare resources are valuable and unique due to limited availability on the market (e.g. people, raw material) or difficult and complex to accumulate within the organization (e.g. social capital, customer relationship).

Figure 3 shows the resource absorption/rarity matrix and the categorization of four different types of slack, by combining the level of absorption and level of rarity, as proposed by Voss *et al.* (2008, p. 149).

Resource Rarity ↓ / Resource Absorption →	low	high
low	**Financial Slack** liquid assets, cash available	**Operational Slack** unused operational resources (excess production capacity)
high	**Customer Relational Slack** relational, committed customers	**Human Resource Slack** specialized, skilled human resources

Figure 3: Resource absorption / rarity matrix
Source: Voss et al. (2008, p. 149)

This approach, distinguishing types of slack by the kind of resource from which they arise, is used by several authors. Often, studies entirely focus on one single type of slack. While e.g. Mellahi and Wilkinson (2010) focuses on HR slack, Lee (2011) and Bradley *et al.* (2011a) investigate solely the effect of financial slack. Yet others, like Mishina *et al.* (2004) simultaneously explore the influence of both HR and financial slack.

As mentioned above, the existing attempts to offer categories for slack are not entirely consistent, and several categories of slack are partially overlapping. Generally, the recoverability of slack plays a major role its categorization. For example the definition of available slack is similar to unabsorbed slack and generated slack, since the main characteristic of both forms is that they are rather easily recoverable and thus offer a high level of flexibility, like e.g. excess liquidity and cash (cf. Krcal, 2012, p. 685). Absorbed slack and invested slack have similar characteristics to low discretion slack and recoverable slack, as those forms of slack are all based on resources that are already committed to specific functions in the organization, therefore recovery is difficult. Regarding the concept of potential slack in matter of the level of discretion, authors hold different views. Some argue that potential sack resembles the form of slack where managers have highest discretion, because additional debt or equity raising potential, e.g. in the form of credit lines, allows for high flexibility (cf. Sharfman *et al.*, 1988, p. 602; Krcal, 2012, pp. 682–683). Others equate potential slack with low discretion slack as it solely presents a future potential and does not allow for immediate deployment (cf. Lin *et al.*, 2009, p. 402; George, 2005, p. 666).

In the empirical part of this study the investigation focuses on financial slack, which refers to excess financial resources, e.g. excess liquidity. This type of slack can be categorized as unabsorbed or available slack, where managerial discretion and thus flexibility of use are rather high.

3.1.2 History of slack in literature

Organizational slack and its effect on organizational phenomena have been discussed in literature for decades. In the following section (1) the origin of slack in literature, (2) frequently cited, early work and (3) recent studies concerning slack are discussed.

(1) The origin

While the foundational concept of slack in literature originates from the 1930s, Cyert and March (1963, p. 42) are credited for the introduction of the label of slack in organizational theory (cf. Sigerstad, 2004, p. 12). In their book "A behavioral theory of the firm", Cyert and March (1963, p. 42) give a first definition[3] of slack, in terms of a surplus in the level of inducements to maintain the coalition. The authors view organizational slack as a result of suboptimal resource allocation.

Generally the authors representing the "Carnegie School of thought" contributed a lot to the early conceptualization of slack. This movement from the 1950s and 1960s includes amongst others the writers Herbert A. Simon, James March, and Richard Cyert. Their work was mainly concerned with the organizational behavior of the firm (cf. Sigerstad, 2004, pp. 13–24).

These authors partly credit Barnard and his inducements-contributions schema from 1938 for the basic idea for slack. The inducements-contributions schema states that equilibrium is required in order to attract and sustain new members in a coalition. In other words, the input and output of resources has to be balanced to ensure survival of an organization (cf. Sigerstad, 2004, p. 13). Barnard did however not specifically apply the term "slack" in his concept (cf. Krcal, 2012, p. 680).

---

[3] See also section 3.1.1 Definition and conceptualization of slack

Another author who contributed to the discussion of resources and growth, and thereby influenced the literature of slack to some extent is the early resource based theorist Penrose (1959) (cf. Mousa, 2009, p. 28; Mishina *et al.*, 2004). The author highlights the importance of a company's resources to achieve competitive advantage. Central aspects to Penrose's growth theory are the use of excess, idle resources as well as managers' entrepreneurial ambition that is the ability to recombine and utilize those resources for growth (cf. Penrose, 1959). This indicates the idea of organizational slack as an opportunity for expansion (cf. Bradley *et al.*, 2011b, p. 537).

(2) Frequently cited, early work

Some papers that are frequently cited in connection with slack literature, also in recent papers, are the studies of Bourgeois (1981), Bourgeois III and Singh (1983), Singh (1986) and Sharfman *et al.* (1988) from the 1980ies (cf. Krcal, 2012, p. 681; Mousa, 2009, pp. 25–27). During that time the main topics concerning slack were to further conceptualize the term and discuss its functions. In addition, several papers focus on the operationalization of slack and engage in first empirical testing.

In the paper "On the Measurement of Organizational Slack", Bourgeois (1981) attempts to categorize the functions of slack and provides suggestions for measurement. He reviews and contrasts various definitions from previous literature, and synthesizes a definition of slack[4] (cf. Mousa, 2009, p. 27). As mentioned before, this definition is used in many recent papers focusing on organizational slack and its effects. In contrast to other authors of his time, Bourgeois holds the view that slack is essential for a company's survival and success (cf. Weidermann, 1984, p. 95).

Bourgeois III and Singh (1983) later apply the financial measures of slack suggested by Bourgeois (1981) in another paper, which is concerned with the effects of slack on strategic and political behavior within top management teams. The authors find that the different types of slack have different effects on political behavior. While potential slack increases political behavior, both available and potential slack reduce goal disagreement. The classifications of slack provided by the authors in this paper, namely available,

[4] *"Organizational slack is that cushion of actual or potential resources which allows an organization to adapt successfully to internal pressures for adjustment or to external pressures for change in policy, as well as to initiate changes in strategy with respect to the external environment." (Bourgeois, 1981, p. 30)*

recoverable and potential slack, are most widely used in slack literature (cf. Cheng and Kesner, 1997, p. 2; Daniel *et al.*, 2004, p. 566).

Singh (1986) is one of the first authors to address the effect of slack on performance, which is one of the most prevalent research topics concerning slack. The author explores the relationship between organizational performance and risk taking, using organizational slack and decentralization as mediators. Singh uses financial measures for slack and hypothesizes that slack is positively associated with performance. He confirms that poor performance is related to low risk taking and the accumulation of slack.

Sharfman *et al.* (1988) investigate the conditions under which slack develops, differentiating between external (from the environment) and internal criteria (from the organization and values/beliefs). They additionally state two requirements - visibility and employability - for resources to be considered slack. The authors argue that excess resources have to be visible and employable in the future in order to turn waste (e.g. resulting from inefficient processes, excess inventory, etc.) into slack. Excess resources can first be considered slack when managers realize their existence and turn them into slack.[5]

Also in German literature slack was a popular research topic at the time. Weidermann (1984) summarizes the findings of well-established English literature about organizational slack. Moreover he provides suggestions for the management, deployment and planning of slack resources. Scharfenkamp (1987) explores how organizational slack influences the organizational structure and is influences by it, as well as the resulting effects on success.

(3) Recent studies (from 1997 to 2012)

Recent studies are regularly concerned with the question whether slack is a strategic tool or an indicator of inefficiency, as well as the search for an optimum level of slack (cf. Sigerstad, 2004, p. 41). Papers studying the strategic effect of slack provide empirical tests on the impact of slack on e.g. innovation, acquisitions, environmental responsiveness, growth, risk attitude, and performance. On the other hand, studies in accounting literature frequently investigate slacks' influence on efficiency, focusing on budgetary slack. Some of the studies concerned with the effects of slack on various

[5] For details on prerequisites see section 3.1.4 Antecedents of slack.

organizational phenomena will be described in more detail in section 3.1.6 Potential utilization of slack.

Overall it can be said that there is a great variety of scholars who performed studies on slack in the last fifty years, therefore in general the concept is well established. However, despite the enormous interest in slack, there is still no broad agreement on its effect on various organizational phenomena. This fact can be explained by having a closer look on the research settings and variables employed in empirical testing. Studies frequently use different classifications for slack and explore the effect of different types of slack. Besides, while some studies focus on the effects of a certain level of slack or attempt to find an optimum level of slack (e.g. Chiu and Liaw, 2009; Nohria and Gulati, 1996), others explore the effects of a reduction or increase of slack, which is the variation in the amount of slack (e.g. Mellahi and Wilkinson, 2010; Love and Nohria, 2005). Furthermore, diverse research settings, sample characteristics and contexts are utilized while various different variables are applied to measure slack (cf. Mousa, 2009, pp. 30–31).

Since the concept of organizational slack is rather well established in literature, slack literature can be categorized as mature. Also the relationship between slack and performance has been studied repeatedly, as will be shown in further detail in section 3.2.2. However partly inconsistent result are provided by authors. Particularly the context of environmental threat has first recently become the focus of various studies. Consequently the author categorizes the relevant theory for this thesis as intermediate.

3.1.3 Role and functions of slack

In the early stages of literature concerning slack March and Simon already highlighted that there are various functions for slack in organizations. The fundamental role of slack is that it allows room for maneuver, both for investing activity and for entrepreneurial behavior. Thus it enables internal and external adaptation processes (cf. March and Simon, 1958, pp. 187–188; Cyert and March, 1963, pp. 42–44).

Bourgeois (1981, p. 31) describe several elementary functions of slack, which are primarily based on its fundamental role - room for maneuver. First they note that slack represents an inducement for organizational actors to remain within the system. Second, the authors mention that slack represents a resource for conflict resolution. Third, they state that it acts as a technical buffering mechanism in the workflow process, and finally the authors argue that slack is a facilitator of certain types of strategic and creative behavior. Several authors, such as Cheng and Kesner (1997, p. 3) and Lin *et al.* (2009, p. 398) seize this concept of functions and distinguish between slack as a resource to exploit opportunities regarding innovation and change and slack as a buffer from external contingencies to counter threats.

In the next section of this thesis, the primary functions of slack (1-3) according to behavioral and resource-based theory are discussed. In addition a frequently debated negative view of slack (4) under agency theory is explained.

(1) Slack as an inducement and a resource for conflict resolution

(2) Slack as a buffer from the external environment

(3) Slack as a facilitator of strategic behavior

(4) Slack as a source for agency problems

(1) Slack as an inducement and a resource for conflict resolution

The function of slack as an inducement is based on the inducement-contribution schema developed and influenced by Barnard (1983), March and Simon (1958), and Cyert and March (1963) (cf. Sigerstad, 2004, pp. 12–13). In their following work Cyert and March (1963, p. 36) define[6] slack as "*payments to members of the coalition in excess of what is required to maintain the organization*". Such payments contain dividends to shareholders, income to employees including bonuses and additional non-monetary factors as well as other benefits to managers that are above the necessary threshold (cf. Weidermann, 1984, p. 14). Therefore slack is the difference between resources which are required to obtain people's contribution and total resources spent in this regard (cf. Bourgeois, 1981, p. 31).

Expanding the concept of slack as an inducement Bourgeois (1981, p. 31) adds the idea of Moch and Pondy, who claim that *"With sufficient slack there will be a solution to every problem […]"* (Moch and Pondy 1977, p. 356, cited in Bourgeois, 1981, p. 31) Conflicts frequently arise between subunits of an organization due to divergent subunit interests and conflicting operational goals (e.g. between sales objectives, inventory goals and

[6] See also section 3.1.1 Definition and conceptualization of slack

production targets). In this context, slack can act as a resource for conflict resolution, as it gives the possibility to address a greater number of goals successively and facilitates decentralized decision making.

Bourgeois III and Singh (1983, p. 44), who deal with the effect of organizational slack on the behavior of management teams, confirm that an increase in recoverable slack reduces political behavior. Thus, recoverable slack prevents conflicts, at least in the short run. In contrast to that, the authors find that potential slack promotes political behavior but inhibits goal conflicts. In other words, potential slack leads to increased formation of coalitions and political behavior, but eventually results in better consensus of long-term goals.

(2) Slack as a buffer from the external environment

Another function of slack is concerned with the attempt to buffer the technical core of an organization from environmental influences. The concept behind this idea is that slack reduces the amount of information that has to be processed and passed on between organizational subunits throughout the workflow (cf. Weidermann, 1984, p. 132). As an example, Bourgeois (1981, p. 31) mentions the attempt to absorb external fluctuations in supplies on the one hand, and demand on the other hand, by establishing inventories at both ends of the production cycle. Consequently the need for tight coordination between procurement and sales is minimized and a constant production flow is ensured. Besides, this function of slack allows a company to absorb inconsistencies between the external environment and the organizational structure, thereby reducing the need for organizational restructuring (cf. Chiu and Liaw, 2009, p. 323).

According to Cheng and Kesner (1997, p. 3) this role of slack is specifically crucial for organizations which are highly affected by an uncontrollable external environment, e.g. during economic recession or external crisis. Hence, as slack provides a resource buffer around the organizations core, conflicting external demands are absorbed and environmental uncertainty can be overcome. However, the authors note that the role of slack as a buffer may result in a weakened responsiveness to changes in the external environment.

Likewise, Sharfman *et al.* (1988, p. 603) address the buffering mechanism of slack and discuss several aspects in which the functions of slack differ from those of other buffers. They argue that slack serves more functions than a mere buffer such as relieving internal pressures and resolving conflicts. Besides, slack is often used under different circumstances such as conflicting external demands, where other buffers are less effective. Finally the authors conclude that, if viewed from a long term perspective, slack functions as a key to survival and long-term effectiveness.

(3) Slack as a facilitator of strategic behavior

A number of studies on organizational slack suggest that one central function of slack is that it enables companies to engage in strategic behavior and to create competitive advantages. As slack provides firms with sufficient resources to exploit external opportunities, it supports growth (cf. Chiu and Liaw, 2009, p. 323).

Additionally, Bourgeois (1981, p. 31) suggests slack supports companies to make modifications to their strategy, as excess resources allow a firm to experiment more safely with new strategies such as the introduction of new products or market entrance strategies. Since slack shields an organization from external risk and protects it from possibly negative project outcomes, experimentation is more accepted when slack is present. Singh (1986, p. 580) agrees with this perspective of slack. His study results confirm that [absorbed] slack is positively related to risk taking. Cheng and Kesner (1997, p. 3) add to the discussion, that firms with excess resources generally respond more aggressively to shifting environmental demands that require action.

A number of recent studies are concerned with the function of slack as a facilitator of strategic behavior. For example Nohria and Gulati (1996) explore the effect of slack on innovation and find that slack resources are a major driver for innovative activities. Besides, Lin *et al.* (2009, p. 399) state that slack increases the ability to adapt to complex competitive landscapes, to launch new initiatives in response to opportunities in new markets or to expand globally. Similarly Tan (2003, pp. 741–742) suggests that slack is particularly beneficial during times of environmental turbulence and uncertainty for companies applying real options strategies.

(4) Slack as a source of agency problems

Opponents of slack suggest that high levels of slack result in agency problems - breeding inefficiencies and inhibiting performance within the organization (cf. Chiu and Liaw, 2009, p. 323). Agency theorists characterize slack as resources that motivate managers to behave in unbeneficial ways. In this regard, excess resources are accumulated by managers in order to serve their own goals or interests (e.g. power, prestige and personal financial gain), which are often not aligned with the company objectives (cf. Tan and Peng, 2003, p. 1251). According to this theory organizational slack promotes administrative behavior while inhibiting entrepreneurial management and thus hindering growth (cf. Bradley *et al.*, 2011b, p. 540).

Authors suggest that, when slack resources are present, suboptimal behavior regarding the strategic performance of a company arises. First of all, only a limited number of strategic alternatives are identified because the search for strategic options is conducted less thoroughly due to the sense of security slack promotes. Moreover, the evaluation of those options is carried out with less scrutiny, making previously unacceptable alternatives appear satisfactory due to the existence of slack. This commonly results in a high rate of failure and the pursuit of pet projects leading to low value adding innovations (cf. Cheng and Kesner, 1997, p. 3; Bourgeois, 1981, p. 31).

Lin *et al.* (2009, p. 404) confirm that [high-discretion] slack leads to suboptimal practices and self-serving decisions among managers. Resulting from high levels of excess resources, managers tend to behave undisciplined, inefficient, and irrationally optimistic. Also George (2005, p. 665) notes that in complex industries slack is frequently perceived as a guarantee for survival, leading to suboptimal instead of performance-maximizing strategic choices.

However, the agency problems associated with excess slack resources can be countered, through entrepreneurial management. Since highly entrepreneurial oriented firms seek and exploit opportunities, the risk of becoming administrative and inward looking is diminished and such firms can use slack to enable growth (cf. Heng and Xiuhao, 2010, p. 3).

In conclusion, slack can have various advantageous but also unfavorable consequences, which partially depend on the type of organizational slack under investigation as well as on the characteristics of the respective firm. Excess slack resources can help to solve conflicts, minimize political behavior, buffer from environmental threats and enable experimentation and strategic behavior (cf. Lee, 2011, pp. 4–50). On the other hand, agency problems, suboptimal behavior and inefficiency can be triggered by the presence of slack (cf. Chiu and Liaw, 2009, p. 324). The more entrepreneurial oriented a firm is, the more beneficial available slack resources can be used (cf. Heng and Xiuhao, 2010, p. 6).

3.1.4 Antecedents of slack

Slack can develop either as the result of a deliberate decision (intended) or as the result of inefficient use of resources (unintended). Intended slack is frequently accumulated deliberately for future use to exploit opportunities arising in the environment, whereas unintended slack generally accrues due to incomplete information about future developments in the environment e.g. a more favorable environment than expected (cf. Scharfenkamp, 1987, p. 62; Krcal, 2012, p. 698). In any case, slack resources must be visible in order to actually be embraced by the term slack. Regarding intended slack, the visibility is basically given. Unintended slack on the other hand first has to be identified (cf. Sharfman *et al.*, 1988, p. 602).

Sharfman *et al.* (1988, pp. 603–611) come up with three categories of conditions that lead to the development of slack, including (1) environmental conditions, (2) the characteristics of the respective organization, and (3) the values and beliefs of the dominant coalition within the organization. The authors frequently distinguish between high and low discretion slack regarding these antecedent categories.

Voss *et al.* (2008, p. 148) also describe possible conditions for the development of slack. However, they only focus on one of the above mentioned categories, namely characteristics of the organizations itself. The authors state that slack is accumulated due to good organizational performance in prior periods, as a planned buffer, or as a result of poor planning.

In this thesis the antecedents of slack are described following the three categories of conditions suggested by Sharfman *et al.* (1988, pp. 603–611).

(1) Environmental conditions

The environmental conditions affecting the development of slack include e.g. the rate and extent of environmental change, the availability of resources, and the structure of the market (cf. Sharfman *et al.*, 1988, p. 603; Krcal, 2012, p. 693).

First, slack develops as a response to changes in the environment (i.e. dynamism). When having sufficient slack available, fluctuations in the environment can be absorbed. The occurrence of environmental change thus stimulates the development of slack. Slow and small changes in the environment can be dealt with, through low discretion slack such as inventory and excess capacity, ensuring a steady production flow. In a rapidly and strongly changing environment, responsiveness is a key factor. Therefore high discretion and available slack such as cash and lines of credit etc. are essential (cf. Sharfman *et al.*, 1988, p. 606). Also the availability of resources on the market (i.e. munificence) influences the amount and type of slack a company holds (cf. Sigerstad, 2004, p. 54). Sharfman *et al.* (1988, p. 606) argue that in growing markets fierce competition leads to resource scarcity. Often specific resources, such as qualified employees and machine capacity are in great demand. Therefore slack is accumulated to avoid the shortage of these resources. In contrast to that, Krcal (2012, p. 694) notes that in terms of resource availability, companies with a fairly easy access to financial resources often carry higher amounts of slack and are less threatened by dynamic environments.

The structure of the market (nature of industry and stage in industry's life cycle) influences which type of slack is likely to accrue. In service companies slack generally develops in the form of high discretion slack (e.g. cash reserves), which is needed to deal with fluctuations in demand and to finance resulting HR activities. In production companies generally physical inventory and machine capacity are essential factors, where advance investments are usually more specific and higher than in service firms. Consequently low discretion slack is more likely to accrue in such firms.

Besides, during the first stages of a company in the industry's life cycle (emergent and growth phase) rapid changes call for high flexibility and low holding costs of resources. Consequently available slack, such as cash and credit commonly develops. When a company enters the maturity phase, efficiency and specific resource requirements result in lower discretion for managers, hence absorbed slack is more likely to occur. Finally, in the decline phase the survival of the company becomes the focus, which is why maximum flexibility next to minimum holding costs is crucial (cf. Sharfman *et al.*, 1988, p. 606). Additionally due to discontinued operations, previously absorbed resources become available again, leading to higher discretion (cf. Krcal, 2012, p. 693).

(2) Organizational characteristics

As characteristics in an organization, which influence the development of slack, Sharfman *et al.* (1988, p. 608) mention size, age, performance, technology and internal stability. First of all, greater size and the resulting higher physical and financial capacity provide a company with more possibilities to accumulate slack. Therefore the larger a company is, the higher the absolute level of slack. Furthermore, a company's age and maturity lead to improved survival skills due to experience and learning. The older a company is the better it is able to predict specific resource needs. This results in the development of higher levels of particular low discretion slack (cf. Sharfman *et al.*, 1988, p. 608). George (2005, p. 665) agrees that the development of slack depends on the company's age and confirms the positive relationship between age and [high-discretion and transient[7]] slack resources. He maintains that young firms often face resource constraints and normally know less about their specific resources requirements.

Regarding performance as a condition for the development of slack, authors principally suggest a positive relationship between the two factors (cf. Sharfman *et al.*, 1988, p. 608; Cyert and March, 1963, p. 138; Voss *et al.*, 2008, p. 148). Accordingly, good performance enables a company to carry higher levels of slack. However, in this regard the environmental conditions such as dynamism of the market have to be taken into account. In a stable environment companies are less likely to hold unnecessary high levels of slack. Therefore Sharfman *et al.* (1988, p. 608) conclude that in calm environments good performance leads to low levels of slack, while in dynamic environments good performance leads to high levels of slack.

The level of technology in a firm is an antecedent for slack, in the way that exceptions occur in the production process. The less predictable a company's technology, the more high discretion slack it will hold. Similarly, the more predictable the requirements for the production process, the more low discretion slack will be required (cf. Sharfman *et al.*, 1988, p. 608; Krcal, 2012, p. 694). With respect to the internal processes of an organization, internal stability affects the development of slack since an unstable internal situation leads to more internal conflicts and increased political behavior among managers. To be able to satisfy various divergent needs a company needs slack resources allowing high discretion (cf. Cyert and March, 1963, p. 42; Sharfman *et al.*, 1988, p. 609).

Majumdar (1998, pp. 379–380) adds to the discussion, that large amounts of slack are typically held by companies who experience soft budget constraints. His research focuses on resource utilization and performance in Indian state owned firms. The author argues that the survival and expan-

---

[7] George (2005, p. 664) defines transient slack as "excess resources available after resource demands for operations have been met." He does not distinguish between high-discretion and low-discretion slack in this definition.

sion of state owned companies is decided and supported by the state, regardless of the capabilities and performance of the respective firm. Hence, inefficiencies and indifference about the performance resulting from the absence of external pressure lead to the development of large amounts of slack resources and wastage in resource utilization.

(3) Values and beliefs of the dominant coalition

The values and beliefs of the dominant coalition are essential for the development of organizational slack, as the decision to acquire or to reduce slack is made collectively. It is important to realize that such management decisions are partly irrational. A collective decision reflects the interests of the dominant coalition including their tendency towards political behavior and risk preferences. Moreover all decisions are influences by organizational culture (cf. Sharfman *et al.*, 1988, p. 609). A key function of the organizational culture is that it shapes the company values and influences their members' decision making and behavior. This includes ethical standards as well as moral practices within the organization. The nature of the organizational culture consequently influences the degree to which slack is created (cf. Dunk and Nouri, 1998, p. 85).

The aspect of political behavior among the dominant coalition has already been addressed in early definition of slack by Cyert and March (1963, p. 42). As discussed before[8], one function of slack is to resolve conflicts. Slack can reduce political behavior by allowing a company to address various interests simultaneously. Therefore the fight over resources between members of the coalition is minimized. As explored by Bourgeois III and Singh (1983), different types of slack have different effects on political behavior. Recoverable slack has a strong negative relationship to political behavior while potential slack has a strong positive relationship. The main reason for the opposite effect is that recoverable slack is already absorbed and therefore not interesting for political behavior, whereas potential slack is highly discretional. Sharfman *et al.* (1988, p. 610) suggest an opposite causal relationship to explain the development of slack. In an organization with strong political behavior a higher level of slack is needed to resolve existing conflicts. Regarding the level of discretion, recoverable slack is primarily present, as it is already absorbed. Available slack on the other hand is subject to political behavior and therefore immediately claimed by managers.

---

[8] See section 3.1.3 Role and functions of slack

Sharfman *et al.* (1988, p. 611) claim that the risk attitude of the dominant coalition, being a collective usually is more extreme than the attitude of single individuals. In opportunity situations the dominant coalition acts risk adverse in order to maintain gains, resulting in higher level of slack. When facing threats the collective becomes more willing to take risks in order to prevent losses, hence the company typically holds less slack.

In summary, it can be said that the development of organizational slack depends on a combination of environmental conditions (e.g. dynamism, munificence, market structure), characteristics of the organization (e.g. age, size, technology, internal stability) and the values and beliefs of the dominant coalition (e.g. risk attitude, tendency towards political behavior). Depending on the specific characteristics of a firm and its environment, different forms of organizational slack are more likely to be accumulated.

3.1.5 Measurement of slack

A great number of studies exist, where one or more measures of organizational slack are used as dependent or independent variables (cf. Daniel *et al.*, 2004, p. 567). However, various different indicators are applied, ranging from public financial data, to ratios based on managers' perceptions gathered through survey data (cf. Lawson, 2001, p. 126). Besides, while some studies use a single measure for slack, others apply multiple measures (cf. Greenley and Oktemgil, 1998, p. 382).

Already in the 1980s the operationalization of slack took a central role in literature, and first empirical tests were performed. In the study "On the Measurement of Organizational Slack" Bourgeois (1981) focuses on the functions of slack and how they can be measured. This work is a theoretical contribution to the discussion of the measurement of slack, as no empirical testing is done. The author suggests the primary use of public financial data and subsequently additionally measurement of slack through collected data directly from the company or its members. Regarding the level of analysis at which to study the functions of slack, several units are proposed. According to the specific research question, individual, sub-unit or organizational levels can be most appropriate. The financial indicators the author recommends include retained earnings, dividend payout, general and administrative expenses, working capital/sales, debt/equity ratio, price/earnings ratio, etc. Some of these measures are among the most frequently applied in recent literature.

Likewise, Marino and Lange (1983, pp. 90–91) are concerned with the measurement of slack. They note that since organizational slack can arise in a variety of forms, the attempt to measure it directly is problematic. Therefore changes are investigated e.g. in comparison to industry financial ratios or previous periods (cf. Marino and Lange, 1983, p. 82). Additionally, a distinction between absolute and relative measures can be made. Absolute measures explore if a company holds a high or low amount of slack compared to its industry or a group of firms. Relative measures on the other hand, examine whether a company is gaining or losing slack over time (cf. Bourgeois, 1981, p. 37, Marino and Lange, 1983, pp. 83–84). The use of relative measures is recommended when a monotone relationship is present between slack and the other variable of interest, and only the direction of change is relevant. Absolute measures are appropriate when the deployment of slack is the focus, implying some threshold level of slack, which permits discretionary use (cf. Marino and Lange, 1983, pp. 90–91).

Bourgeois (1981, p. 37) makes another distinction between indicators for slack generated from internal and external sources. Changes in internal sources of slack are created by management and actively influenced by managerial policy. This includes e.g. retained earnings, dividend payout and working capital. External sources of slack are induced through external factors, such as the firm's credit rating, stock price / earnings ratio, etc.

Later, Bourgeois III and Singh (1983) apply the financial indicators previously suggested by Bourgeois (1981, p. 30) using financial data from annual reports to examine the effect of slack on strategic and political behavior. They use relative measures, detecting the change in the amount of slack resources from the previous year and distinguishing between slack gaining and slack losing conditions. The authors show that different types of slack and hence different measures of slack effect strategic behavior differently.

Two methods of measuring slack are well established in the literature. Some authors use survey data based on managerial assessments, collected e.g. through questionnaires or interviews, while others rely on financial data. Both approaches have their advantages, as pointed out in the following section (cf. Lin *et al.*, 2009, p. 402). Studies using managerial assessments of slack resources include e.g. Nohria and Gulati (1996), Tan and Peng (2003), Heng and Xiuhao (2010) and Elmassri and Harris (2011).

Nohria and Gulati (1996) collect survey data through a self-report questionnaire from functional department managers at subsidiaries of two major multinational corporations. They measure slack based on estimates of how much the participants would expect to be affected by sudden changes e.g. in operating budget or working time. Similarly Tan and Peng (2003), as well as Heng and Xiuhao (2010), use a survey questionnaire for data collection. Distinguishing between two types of slack, the authors ask for an assessment on whether firms have been operating below engineered capacity for measuring absorbed slack. Unabsorbed slack is measured based on whether a firm has sufficient retained earnings for market expansion, whether a pool of financial resources is available for discretionary use, and whether the firm is able to secure necessary bank loans. Elmassri and Harris (2011) on the other hand, apply a case study method and conduct structured interviews in a state owned Egyptian firm. The predetermined interview questions focus on the aspects budgetary participation, information asymmetry, budget emphasis and propensity to create slack. Additionally, several questions concerning behavioral aspects are asked.

An advantage of studies based on managerial assessments is that complex relationships can be explored, which are not easily allegeable through a simple causal model or by statistical tests (cf. Elmassri and Harris, 2011, p. 281). A frequent problem however is that managerial assessments are based on subjective estimates of individuals, which highly depend on participants' perception. Managers may not be able to accurately assess the situation or may not be willing to make such a revelation, which may lead to biased results (cf. Sigerstad, 2004, p. 44; Nohria and Gulati, 1996, p. 1253).

Studies applying financial ratios from publicly available data are more frequently found in recent literature (cf. Lin *et al.*, 2009, p. 402). When using measures for slack based on financial data the issue of perceptional differences can be avoided. While such measures are more objective and readily available, they may provide less rich and profound information.

Lin *et al.* (2009, p. 402) state that the most commonly used financial indicators for slack are current ratio and debt/equity ratio. Likewise Daniel *et al.* (2004), who performed a meta-analysis based 66 prior studies, find that the majority of studies exploring available slack apply current ratio as an indicator. Besides, more than half of the studies under investigation relating to potential slack apply either debt/equity ratio or equity/debt ratio as an indicator.Table 2 gives an overview of the types of slack investigated, applied measurement and context of several recent studies of organizational slack based on financial data.

Author(s)	Year	Type of Slack	Measures	Context
Vanacker, T., Collewaert, V. and Paeleman, I.	2013	financial (1) human resource (1)	cash + cash equivalents / assets employment cost / assets	performance venture capital and angel investors
Lin, W.-T. and Liu, Y.	2012	n/a	current ratio equity / debt ratio	internationalization
Bradley, S.W., Shepherd, D.A. and Wiklund, J.	2011	available (1)	cash reserve	performance tough environment
Bradley, S.W., Wiklund, J. and Shepherd, D.A.	2011	financial (1)	WC available - WC required*	growth entrepreneurial management
Lee, S.	2011	available (1) potential (1)	current ratio debt / equity ratio	performance
Modi, S.B. and Mishra, S	2011	n/a	inventory, production, and marketing efficiency	performance efficiency
Mellahi, K. and Wilkinson, A.	2010	human resource (1)	sales per employee	innovation downsizing and slack reduction
Wefald, A.J., et. al.	2010	absorbed (1) available (1)	G&A** / sales gross profit - net profit / sales	performance outliers
Wefald, A.J., et. al.	2010	absorbed (1) available (1)	G&A** / sales gross profit - net profit / sales	performance role of industry
Chiu, Y.-C. and Liaw, Y.-C.	2009	available (1) recoverable (1) potential (1)	current ratio SG&A*** / sales equity / debt ratio	performance strategic orientation
Ju, M. and Zhao, H.	2009	absorbed (1) unabsorbed (1)	SG&A*** / sales quick ratio	performance ownership and competitive intensity
Latham, S.F. and Braun, M.R.	2009	available (1)	current ratio	performance economic recession
Lin, W.-T., Cheng, K.-Y. and Liu, Y.	2009	high-discretion (1) low-discretion (1)	curret ratio equity / debt ratio	internationalization
Su, Z., Xie, E. and Li, Y.	2009	unabsorbed (2)	net current assets / assets assets / debt ratio	performance institutional transition

Author(s)	Year	Type of Slack	Measures	Context
Iyer, D.N. and Miller, K.D.	2008	absorbed (1) unabsorbed (1) potential (1)	SG&A*** / sales current ratio debt / equity ratio	performance acquisitions
Voss, G.B., Sirdeshmukh, D. and Voss, Z.G.	2008	financial (1) customer relational (1) operational (1) human resouce (1)	cash reserve subscription revenue unutilized capacity % of full-time staff	product exploration and exploitation environmental threat
Herold, D.M., Jayaraman, N. and Narayanaswamy, C.R.	2006	unabsorbed, available (1)	quick ratio	innovation
Martinez, R.J. and Kendall, A.	2006	available (1) potential (1)	current ratio debt / equity ratio	risk-taking
George, G.	2005	high-discretion (1) low-discretion (1) transient (2)	cash reserve debt / equity ratio resource availability resource demand	performance privately held companies
Love, G.E. and Nohria, N.	2005	absorbed (1)	SG&A*** / sales	performance downsizing
Mishina, Y., Pollock, T.G. and Porac, J.F.	2004	financial (1) human resource (1)	WC available - WC required* employees / sales	growth
Tan, J. and Peng, M.W.	2003	absorbed (3) unabsorbed (5)	major repair fund inventory fund accounts payable depreciation fund reserve fund loan capacity sales expenses retained earnings	performance state owned enterprises economic transition

( ) = number of measures employed
*WC available = cash, cash equivalents, inventory, accounts receivable; WC required = accounts payable, accrued expenses
**G&A = general and administrative expenses
***SG&A = sales, general and administrative expenses

Table 2: Overview of financial indicators of slack

The recent studies from 2003 to 2012 shown in Table 2 underpin the mentioned findings of Daniel *et al.* (2004).

Nine of the listed studies employ current ratio or quick ratio as an indicator for available, high discretion or unabsorbed slack. This is more than half of the 14 studies that are concerned with these forms of slack. Furthermore, all of the seven studies investigating potential or low-discretion slack employ debt/equity or equity/debt ratio as an indicator. General and administrative expenses divided by sales or sales, general and administrative expenses divided by sales are a common indicator for absorbed or recoverable slack, employed in six of the seven studies that examine these forms of slack.

Other common measures for slack include cash reserve, which was used three times for available, financial and high discretion slack, as well as resources availability minus resource demand e.g. in the form of working capital, which was used three times for financial or transient slack. For human resource slack, sales per employee or reversed (total number of employees divided by sales) and the percentage of full time staff are commonly used.

When looking at the indicators employed it becomes clear once more that there is a certain amount of overlap among the classifications and measures of slack (cf. Mousa, 2009, p. 40; Moses, 1992, p. 59). For instance, the current ratio was utilized as a measure of unabsorbed slack, available slack, and generated slack. While debt/equity ratio or inverted was used as an indicator for both potential and low discretion slack. In addition, when studying the effect of slack on organizational aspects such as performance, it is important to be aware of the fact that the measure employed for slack as well as performance has a crucial influence on the outcome of the study (cf. Sigerstad, 2004, p. 44).

3.1.6 Potential utilization of slack

In order to discuss potential ways of deployment of slack it is necessary to take a closer look at the prerequisites for the utilization of slack in general. In the literature the ability to plan slack, its visibility and its employability are suggested as factors that are crucial for the utilization of slack.

First, as previously discussed, organizational slack can develop intended if it is generated deliberately for future use (i.e. planned), or unintended if it is accumulated unknowingly as a result of incomplete information (cf.

Scharfenkamp, 1987, p. 62; Krcal, 2012, p. 698). Second, irrespective of the ability to plan slack it must be visible to managers in order to be used. This visibility implies that slack is identifiable and measureable. While intended slack is visible by definition, unintended slack has to be identified first (cf. Sharfman *et al.*, 1988, p. 602). Finally employability, which refers to the availability of slack in the future, is essential. Depending on where slack is located within a company, slack resources have to be either available or recovered before they can be deployed for any purpose (cf. Krcal, 2012, p. 700). When these conditions are present, slack can be deployed for a variety of strategic purposes. As mentioned in section 3.1.2 History of slack in literature, recent studies on slack resources examine its effect on (1) innovation, (2) acquisitions and internationalization, (3) growth, (4) risk taking, and (5) performance. These potential purposes of utilization of slack are discussed in this section.

(1) Innovation

Two authors that strongly influenced the literature about the link between slack and innovation are Nohria and Gulati. They argue that on the one hand slack facilitates experimentation while on the other hand it diminishes discipline over innovative projects, resulting in an inverse U-shaped relationship. Correspondingly, the authors suggest that there is an optimum level of slack in every organization (cf. Nohria and Gulati, 1996; Nohria and Gulati, 1997). Herold *et al.* (2006) extend Nohria and Gulati's (1996) studies on slack and innovation by using various measures for bot variables for a cross-sectional sample and two time periods. They find support for the suggestion of a curvilinear relationship and the existence of an optimum level of slack (cf. Herold *et al.*, 2006, p. 384). Heng and Xiuhao (2010, p. 3) examine the unfavorable impact of slack on innovation in the light of entrepreneurial orientation. They conclude that high entrepreneurial orientation in a firm enables the efficient use of slack resources for innovation. Hence the disadvantages of slack, promoting undisciplined innovation activities and the investment in pet projects, are reduced by entrepreneurial management.

Katila and Shane (2005) investigate the innovativeness of new firms based on their lack of resources, taking into account environmental conditions. They argue along the contingency theory that the value of resources heavily depends on the context in which they are used, namely the environment in which the company is operating. In other words, the level of resources alone is not sufficient to determine if a company is innovative. In fact the authors state that the external environment heavily influences the value of resources and therefore their effect on innovation.

The call for a more contextual approach is answered e.g. by Voss *et al.* (2008) and Zona (2012). The results of Voss *et al.* (2008) show that under external threat, unabsorbed slack is positively connected with exploration but negatively with exploitation. This implies that in times of crisis companies follow offensive strategies and use slack to counter threats and allow for long term success. However, when environmental threat is low, risk is generally avoided and financial and customer relational slack is rather preserved which inhibits product exploration but fuels product exploitation. Zona (2012) comes to a similar conclusion. The author points out a dilemma that arises during a crisis. While the reduction of risk and investment can be essential for short term survival, increased risk taking and investments in innovation is vital to ensure competitive advantage and long term success. The study results show that slack resources provide protection against unfavorable events resulting in less risk aversion. Correspondingly a higher amount of slack leads to more innovation investment during crisis.

In summary, several studies highlight the beneficial view of slack regarding innovation. Yet, while slack can be used to increase innovation, it bears the threat of inefficient or undisciplined investment. This disadvantageous use of slack can be reduced by entrepreneurial orientation. Additionally, the environment influences the effect of slack on innovation. When external threat or crisis are present, slack (particularly unabsorbed slack) increases risk taking and leads to more innovation and product exploration enabling long-term performance and future growth.

(2) Acquisitions and internationalization

Iyer and Miller (2008) and Lin *et al.* (2009) provide similar arguments concerning the impact of slack on acquisitions. They agree that high amounts of unabsorbed slack result in increased engagement in acquisition and activities and market expansion. The authors argue that when reaching a sufficient level, slack is perceived as a buffer for the risk related to the acquisition and integration of another firm. Likewise, slack facilitates the search and generates opportunities for change, resulting in more experimentation, acquisitions and increased internationalization activities. Thus, Iyer and Miller (2008, p. 811) conclude that unabsorbed slack is a major driver for acquisitions. However, Lin *et al.* (2009, p. 404) point out that at lower levels, slack can inhibit internationalization due to irrational optimism and self-interested decisions of managers. Therefore they suggest a U-shaped relationship between high discretion slack and internationalization.

Wan and Yiu (2009) apply an environmental perspective on the relationship and note that slack becomes especially beneficial during environmental jolts, when resources are scarce. Hence, in a threatening external environment unabsorbed slack positively influences performance and acquisition activities, irrespectively of the amount. The authors state that the negative impact of slack, suggested e.g. by Lin *et al.* (2009, p. 404) dissolves during environmental jolts. In other words, in a munificent environment slack can lead to irrational optimism and self-interested decisions (such as inappropriate, overpriced acquisitions), but when environment is resource scarce slack becomes a crucial factor for acquisitions and performance.

Patzelt *et al.* (2008) focus their investigation on the utilization of slack to form new strategic alliances. They state that high discretion financial slack is viewed as a substitute for alliances, resulting in a direct negative relationship. Generally managers seem to prefer internally controlled resources over external resources. When examining non-financial capabilities as an intervening variable, the situation differs. Managers, who have high discretion financial slack at their disposal, commonly attempt to compensate weaknesses in their company's existing capabilities through alliances. Consequently high levels of financial slack lead to an active search for the formation of new strategic alliances in case a firm has weaknesses in its existing capabilities.

In conclusion, unabsorbed slack such as financial slack leads to more acquisition and internationalization activities, especially if it is available in high levels. Similar to the potential disadvantageous effect of slack on innovation, it can also lead to inefficiencies and unfavorable acquisitions. However during environmental threat or crisis the effect of slack on acquisitions becomes increasingly positive. Besides, when a weakness is perceived in a firm's capabilities, financial slack enables a firm to compensate through alliances.

(3) Growth

Following Penrose's growth theory and the idea that idle resources as well as the recombination of existing resources provide an opportunity for firm growth, Bradley *et al.* (2011b) investigate the slack-growth link. They find that financial slack positively effects growth through the exploitation of current resources, while high levels of financial slack inhibit entrepreneurial management and lead to lower exploration of new opportunities. They conclude that this demonstrates the dual effect of slack on growth. On the one hand growth is boosted through the use of idle resources and traditional means like market expansion, while on the other hand it is inhibited because of less creative recombination of existing resources (cf. Bradley *et al.*, 2011b, pp. 548–549). The results of Voss *et al.* (2008) basically support these findings. However, when additionally considering the external environment, the authors report that the relationship reverses. Under threat, managers become more risk seeking, entrepreneurial oriented and foster the exploration of new opportunities, while product exploitation becomes secondary.

Mishina *et al.* (2004) examine the effect of slack on short term sales growth in a sample of manufacturing companies, managed by successful entrepreneurs. Their results show that different types of slack have essentially differing effects. While financial slack facilitates product expansion, human resource slack inhibits it. On the other hand, market expansion is facilitated by HR slack. The authors conclude that expansion strategies alone are not directly related to growth (cf. Mishina *et al.*, 2004, p. 1191).

The above mentioned studies point out once more that slack can impact a firm negatively. By inhibiting entrepreneurial management and thus reducing the exploration of new opportunities slack impedes growth. However, when facing external threat, the arguments of authors studying the implications of slack for growth support a beneficial view of slack.

(4) Risk taking

As mentioned before, Singh (1986) provide evidence that slack encourages risk taking. Specifically he argues that good performance increases the level of slack, which subsequently promotes risk taking. Moses, 1992 draws upon the work of Singh (1986) and investigates risk taking in terms of product pricing strategies. The author confirms that increased organizational slack results in more risky strategic decisions concerning product pricing, since slack buffers from failure. Likewise, the results of Martinez and Kendall (2006) confirm that generally in a competitive environment, high levels of available slack as well as potential slack induce risk taking. They argue that when competition is high, companies use slack as a buffer from poor performance.

Voss *et al.* (2008) as well as Zona (2012) also account for the association of slack and risk taking in their study of the slack-innovation link. Zona

(2012, p. 54) shows that past successes lead to a stronger risk seeking attitude of the CEO, but this effect is contingent on organizational slack resources. Voss *et al.* (2008) focus on the interaction between the external environment and risk taking. The authors point out that environmental threat leads to higher risk seeking behavior and the deployment of slack for investments in product exploration, while in calm environments risk is generally avoided and slack is conserved.

Overall authors agree that slack induces risk taking behavior. However, the question of the resulting effect on performance is unanswered. While some authors investigating risk taking behavior stress the negative impact of risk taking on performance. Others perceive risk taking as a crucial factor to enable competitive advantage, performance and long term success.

(5) Performance

One of the most frequently discussed topics regarding organizational slack is its influence on performance. A great number of studies investigate how slack resources can be deployed to improve performance, using various measures and contexts. Besides, the variables and associations from the above mentioned studies of slack (with innovation, risk taking, growth, etc.) can be viewed as intervening variables between slack and performance. However, they do not give direct evidence on the slack-performance link (cf. Mousa, 2009, p. 31).

Daniel *et al.* (2004) provide a meta-analysis of previous studies, reviewing 80 samples from 66 studies on relationship between slack and performance. They note that generally a positive effect of slack on performance is found. Tan (2003) and Tan and Peng (2003) criticize that the slack-performance link has previously only been tested in developed economies and suggest that the environmental context plays an important role. Later Su *et al.* (2009) and Ju and Zhao (2009) both replicate and extend the work of Tan and Peng (2003). Su *et al.* (2009) examine the moderating effect of the environmental factors munificence and dynamism on the relationship between slack and performance and Ju and Zhao (2009) suggest that the relationship is moderated by ownership type and competitive intensity in the environment. Other authors that take certain environmental factors into consideration are e.g. Latham and Braun (2009) and Bradley *et al.* (2011a). Latham and Braun (2009) explore the slack-performance link during economic downturn and recession, while Bradley *et al.* (2011a) investigate the role of slack in connection with value creation and performance, laying a special focus on environmental dynamism and munificence. George (2005) attempts to apply the findings from previous studies of publicly traded firms, on privately held firms, while Wefald *et al.* (2010b) study the performance effect of slack, specifically controlling for industry type. Additionally, Wefald *et al.* (2010a) point out that the impact of outliers is one factor that partially explains previously reported contradictory results. Other authors, who are concerned with the utilization of slack to improve performance, are e.g. Greenley and Oktemgil (1998), Lee (2011), Chiu and Liaw (2009), Vanacker *et al.* (2013), Modi and Mishra (2011), and Love and Nohria (2005).

The existing theories and investigations of the association of slack with performance relationship will be discussed in more detail in section 3.2 The relationship between slack and performance.

All in all, a great variety of scholars performed studies on the utilization of slack and its effect on organizational phenomena. When comparing the results it has to be noted that different types and levels of slack have different effects and lead to different strategic actions. Although there is still no broad agreement, the majority of authors view slack as beneficial. Particularly the influence of environmental factors provides valuable perspectives on organizational slack.

Several authors suggest that the lack of evidence for the successful utilization of slack resources is due to the lack of consistency in the research design, measurement of variables and techniques of analysis. For instance, different and partially overlapping classifications for slack as well as different types of slack are used to explore its effects. Furthermore, various variables are applied to measure slack as well as the other variable of interest (e.g. innovation, risk taking or performance) and different moderator variables are used. In addition, diverse sample characteristics and contexts are utilized (cf. Mousa, 2009, pp. 30–31; Greenley and Oktemgil, 1998, pp. 382–383).

3.2 The relationship between slack and performance

The focus of this study lies on the link between slack and performance. This has been a popular research topic in recent as well as in earlier literature. As elaborated above, two contrasting perspectives on slack (resource based view and behavioral theory vs. agency theory) are present. Studies have shown that the specific results on the effect of slack on performance is highly dependent on the measures and types of slack used, as well as the context in which the relationship is studied.

3.2.1 Definition of performance

Before looking at the influence slack resources have on performance in more detail, it is essential to define the term performance in this context and determine how performance is measured.

This thesis examines the financial performance of organizations, which can be broadly described as a measure of change in the financial condition of a firm. In this regard, an organization is viewed as a voluntary association of human, physical and capital resources, aiming to achieve a particular common objective. The financial outcome in an organization results from management decisions and their implementation. To a large extent, the collective purpose of the organization determines what the desired outcome is. Correspondingly, neither in literature nor in practice an agreement on the best measures for performance exists. Instead, the definition of performance is generally governed by the underlying theory and research purpose (cf. Carton and Hofer, 2007, pp. 2–7).

The construct of performance can be broken down into multiple dimensions, e.g. financial, operational or stakeholder dimension. In this thesis, the financial performance is of interest. However, a variety of interacting subcategories of financial performance exist, e.g. profitability, growth, efficiency, liquidity, etc. When a firm shows good performance in one of the categories, this might affect another performance metric negatively. For instance, a firm might sacrifice profitability or efficiency in the short term in order to boost long term growth or ensure survival (cf. Carton and Hofer, 2007, pp. 56–58).

Various ways of measurement are proposed for the different dimensions of performance by previous authors. Just as no ideal measure for overall organizational performance is agreed upon, no measurement model that accurately represents the multiple dimensions of the performance construct exists (cf. Carton and Hofer, 2007, p. 25). Instead, the best definition of a metric for performance always depends on the specific purpose of measurement and the decision the metric should support (cf. Losbichler *et al.*, 2012, p. 125). The large variety of suggested measures can be divided into several categories, as shown in Figure 4.

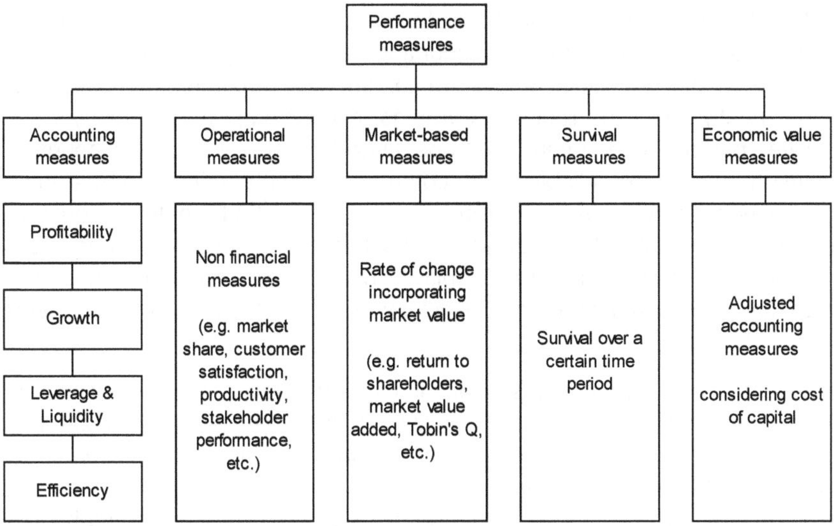

Figure 4: Categories of Performance Measures adapted from Carton and Hofer (2007, pp. 61–63)

In this thesis an accounting measure is used to determine the financial performance of the sample firms. Accounting measures are based upon the financial statements of a company and generally represent ratios or percentages for past financial performance.

Several subcategories exist for accounting measures, as presented in the figure above (cf. Carton and Hofer, 2007, p. 63). More precisely, in this thesis profitability is measured. Profitability ratios are based on companies' earnings (such as net income, operating income, or earnings before tax) and capital required for the generation of those earnings (cf. Losbichler *et al.*, 2012, p. 125). Profitability measures are among the most commonly used measures to assess the financial performance of a company (cf. Carton and Hofer, 2007, p. 82).

Accounting measures for profitability have several limitations. The main issue is that different accounting principles exist (e.g. US GAAP, IFRS, and various national GAAP). These accounting principles generally allow the use of alternative and equally accepted accounting methods for similar transactions. Thus, for instance earnings figures can be calculated in various ways.

Although generally a certain consistency is required once an accounting method is chosen, changes in accounting methods might occur under specific circumstances. Such a change for financial reporting purposes can substantially affect the reported earnings, even though the company's objective performance might be unchanged. Consequently, accounting measures can be unreliable when compared between different firms and / or between different years (cf. Venanzi, 2012, p. 2). Additionally, accounting measures are subject to managerial discretion and reporting dates. Estimates made by managers can significantly affect earnings and accounting measures of performance (cf. Losbichler *et al.*, 2012, p. 126; Carton and Hofer, 2007, p. 67).

In this thesis return on assets (ROA) is used to determine the financial performance of the sample firms. Basically, ROA measures an organization's ability to utilize its assets to create performance, expressed as a percentage of profit that a firm earned in relation to its overall assets. ROA is chosen to measure financial performance because several authors emphasize that this measure is widely used and most appropriate to operationalize performance in comparison to slack (cf. Lee, 2011, p. 10; Chiu and Liaw, 2009, p. 328). Other indicators for performance in slack research are profit values like EBIT, gross profit and pre-tax profit as well as ratios like ROE, ROI and ROS[9]. One advantage of profitability ratios like ROA is that they do not solely measure profitability in terms of earnings, but in reference to the capital required (cf. Losbichler *et al.*, 2012, p. 125).

Various formulas for the calculation of the measure ROA exist in the literature. Although several studies emphasize that ROA is widely used in slack literature (cf. Lee, 2011, p. 10; Chiu and Liaw, 2009, p. 328), authors apply different definitions of the metric. Moreover, some authors use ROA as a performance metric, but do not state the exact definition applied (e.g. Latham and Braun, 2009; Chiu and Liaw, 2009; Greenley and Oktemgil, 1998). The standard definition of ROA is net income divided by total assets. One problem with this definition is that the nominator and denominator are not fully comparable. The interest expense has to be added to the net income when compared to total assets, since it has been generated through the total assets in the same period (cf. Losbichler *et al.*, 2012, p. 125). The

---

[9] See Table 3 for a review of applied measures for performance in recent studies

standard definition also does not specify whether extraordinary P/L such as restructuring charges, unusual or nonrecurring items and results from discontinued operations should be included. Besides, profit before tax instead of net income can be applied in order to cancel out any taxation differences as well as extraordinary P/L (cf. Krause and Arora, 2010, p. 41). Some authors on the other hand focus on operating profit before interest, taxes, depreciation and amortization, thereby excluding e.g. differences in the capital structure of firms (e.g. Love and Nohria, 2005; Ju and Zhao, 2009). Each of these definitions has its advantages. In this study, the following three definitions of ROA are applied in order to demonstrate the implications of differing definitions.

$$ROA_{ni} = \frac{\text{Net Income}}{\text{Total Assets}}$$

$$ROA_{pre\text{-}tax} = \frac{\text{P/L before tax}}{\text{Total Assets}}$$

$$ROA_{EBITDA} = \frac{\text{EBITDA*}}{\text{Total Assets}}$$

* EBITDA = Earnings before interest, taxes, depreciation and amortization

It has to be noted that ROA differs considerably across industries, not only because of different accounting policies, but also due to differences in firms' capital intensity, financial structures, and average amount of total assets (cf. Carton and Hofer, 2007, pp. 84–85). Since one single industry from a specified region is investigated in this thesis, the effects of industry differences are eliminated. Furthermore, to minimize the problem of differing accounting methods to some extent in this thesis, only firms reporting consolidated IFRS financial statements are included in the sample.

3.2.2 Theories and findings on the relationship

As mentioned before, the association between slack and performance is the topic of a great number of studies in early as well as recent literature. Daniel *et al.* (2004) review and compare previous studies concerned with slack and performance. They report that existing results on the relationship are somewhat inconclusive. The findings of the reviewed studies show partial support for a positive linear, negative linear as well as curvilinear relationship between slack and performance. Likewise recent studies indicate mixed results. While some recent authors (e.g. Bradley *et al.*, 2011a; Lee, 2011; Su *et al.*, 2009) find a positive linear relationship other authors (e.g. Ju and Zhao, 2009; Tan and Peng, 2003) report a negative association of performance with some types of slack and yet others (e.g. Wefald *et al.*, 2010a; Chiu and Liaw, 2009; Love and Nohria, 2005) argue that a curvilinear relationship exists.

A problem which contributes to this inconsistency of results is the fact that the used samples and measurements differ widely. Furthermore, different slack types, like available, recoverable and potential slack, interact differently with performance measures (cf. Daniel *et al.*, 2004, p. 565; Sigerstad, 2004, p. 44). In addition, methodological issues exist among previous studies. While some authors apply one measure, others use multiple measures for slack and / or performance (cf. Greenley and Oktemgil, 1998, p. 378).

The results of Daniel *et al.'s* (2004, pp. 571–572) meta-analysis, which is based on 80 samples of US firms, overall show a positive influence of slack on performance. This supports the arguments of behavioral theory and resource based view that slack is a valuable resource which can be used as a strategic tool. The authors highlight that the type of slack used has a significant influence on the strength of the slack-performance relationship. Since available and potential slack are readily deployable and allow for high managerial discretion, those slack resources have a stronger influence on performance. Recoverable or absorbed slack on the other hand, is harder to access and therefore does not affect performance in the same extent.

Table 3 presents recent studies from 1998 to 2012 concerned with the association of slack and performance. Specifically it shows which types of slack were examined, how many and which measures were used, in which context the relationship was studied and what the main findings were.

	Author(s)	Year	Types of Slack	Measures of Slack	Measures of Perfor.	Moderator / Context	Findings
1	Vanacker, T., Collewaert, V. and Paeleman, I.	2013	financial (1) human resource (1)	cash + cash equivalents / assets employment cost / assets	gross profit	venture capital and angel investors, ownership stakes	positive relationship: angel investors increase the value of slack; HR slack has a more positive effect on performance
2	Bradley, S.W., Shepherd, D.A. and Wiklund, J.	2011	available (1)	cash reserve	EBIT	environmental munificence and dynamism	positive relationship: strongest for low munificence and low dynamism environment
3	Lee, S.	2011	available (1) potential (1)	current ratio debt / equity	ROA		positive for available and potential slack; stronger for available slack and small firms
4	Modi, S.B. and Mishra, S	2011		inventory, production, and marketing efficiency	Stock-Returns Tobin's Q ROA		resource efficiency improvements positively influence firms stock returns, Tobins Q and ROA but with diminishing returns
5	Wefald et. al.	2010	absorbed (1) available (1)	G&A** / sales gross profit - net profit / sales	ROA ROE	outliers	measurement of slack / performance and outliers affect results
6	Wefald et. al.	2010	absorbed (1) available (1)	G&A** / sales gross profit - net profit / sales	ROA ROE APL*		mixed results: curvilinear ∩ for absorbed and available slack partially supported
7	Chiu, Y.-C. and Liaw, Y.-C.	2009	available (1) recoverable (1) potential (1)	current ratio SG&A*** / sales equity / debt	ROA ROE ROIC	strategy (product scope, vertical integration and R&D intensity)	curvilinar ∩ for available and potential slack curvilinear ∪ for recoverable slack
8	Ju, M. and Zhao, H.	2009	absorbed (1) unabsorbed (1)	SG&A*** / sales quick ratio	ROA	ownership and competitive intensity	negative for absorbed slack positive for unabsorbed slack
9	Latham, S.F. and Braun, M.R.	2009	available (1)	current ratio	ROA	economic recession	slack associated with steeper rate of decline but faster rate of recovery
10	Su, Z., Xie, E. and Li, Y.	2009	unabsorbed (2)	net current assets / assets assets / debt	ROA	institutional transition; dynamism and munificence	positive realtionship
11	Love, G.E. and Nohria, N.	2005	absorbed (1)	SG&A*** / sales	ROA-market ROA-book	Downsizing: scope of downsizing, proactive or reactive timing	generally curvilinar ∩: proactive or broadly scoped downsizings more successful than reactive and narrowly scoped

	Author(s)	Year	Types of Slack	Measures of Slack	Measures of Perfor.	Moderator / Context	Findings
12	George, G.	2005	high-discret.(1) low-discret. (1) transient (2)	cash reserve debt / equity resource availability resource demand	gross profit	privately held firms; firm age and industry complexity	mixed results: positive linear for high discretion slack; curvilinar ∩ for low discretion slack; transient unlikely to enhance performance
13	Tan, J. and Peng, M.W.	2003	absorbed (1) unabsorbed (3)	capacity utilization retained earnings discretionary fund debt financing	ROA market position	state owned enterprises economic transition	mixed results: mostly negative for absorbed slack; positive for unabsorbed slack
14	Tan, J. and Peng, M.W.	2003	absorbed (3) unabsorbed (5)	major repair fund inventory fund accounts payable depreciation fund reserve fund loan capacity sales expenses retained earnings	pre-tax profits	state owned enterprises economic transition	mixed results: negative for absorbed slack positive for unabsorbed slack curvilinear ∩ relationship
15	Greenley, G.E. and Oktemgil, M.	1998	generated (6) invested (4)	CF / investment, debt / equity EBIT / interest cover Market / book value Current ratio Sales per employee Admin. exp. / sales Dividend payout Sales / total assets WC / sales	ROE ROI RONA ROS		mixed results: high performing: many positive associations low performing: few positive associations positive association mainly exists for high performing companies

( ) = number of measures employed
*APL = average worker productivity (sales / workers)
**G&A = general and administrative expenses
***SG&A = sales, general and administrative expenses

Table 3: Review of recent studies on the slack-performance link

This review of recent studies shows various inconsistencies, which largely correspond to the concerns previously pointed out by Daniel *et al.* (2004) and Greenley and Oktemgil (1998). The main issues, which the review of studies shows are (1) differences in types of slack examined, (2) differences in measures for slack and performance, (3) differences concerning the sample, as well as (4) differences concerning the context.

(1) Differences in types of slack examined

In the listed studies various types of slack are examined. Unabsorbed and absorbed, available, recoverable, and potential, generated and invested, transient as well as financial and human resource slack are all common classifications of organizational slack. It is important to note that there is a strong overlap between the categories used for types of slack. For a better overview the distinct forms of slack can be subsumed in two main pools along the dimension of recoverability.

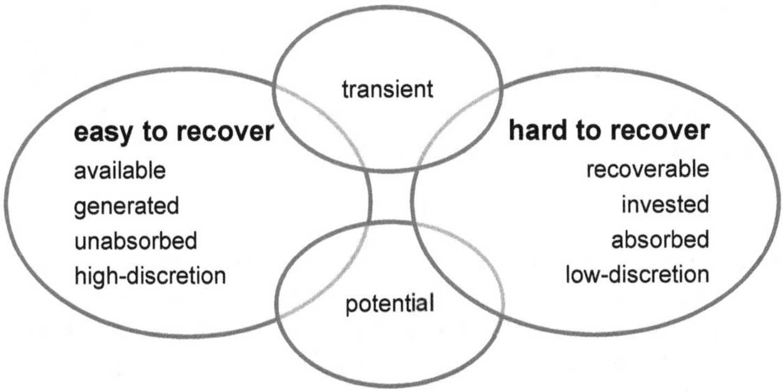

Figure 5: Pools of slack categories corresponding to the dimension of recoverability

The types of slack in each pool share similar characteristics. While the easy to recover types of slack are currently not committed to specific operations and can be deployed rather easily, the hard to recover types are integrated into the company's system and therefore less flexible in their utilization. Potential and transient slack can feature characteristics of both forms, which is why they are represented in separate circles. For definitions of the specific types see section 3.1.1 Definition and conceptualization of slack.

Taking a look at the two main pools of slack and their influence on performance according to the listed studies, partially mixed results are present. Thirteen out of the fifteen studies listed in Table 3 investigates some type of slack that is easy to recover. Out of these, eight studies find a positive relationship between slack and performance, while two studies report an inverse U-shaped, and three studies provide mixed results. Therefore it can be said that generally easily recoverable and readily available slack is a valuable resource to improve performance. That is, this type of slack has a beneficial effect on performance.

On the other hand, ten studies include measures for some of the hard to recover types of slack. In this context, the findings of the studies are rather conflictive. While three studies report a negative effect of slack on performance, one study reports a positive impact and two studies report mixed results. Four other studies find a curvilinear relationship, whereof one states a U-shaped relationship while three studies report an inverse U-shaped connection. As these results show, there is less agreement concerning the effect of not readily available slack on performance. This may be due to the fact that those types of slack can be absorbed in different business operations, resulting in various effects on performance.

(2) Differences in measures of slack and performance

Another difference among the reviewed studies, which leads to inconsistent results, is that some authors use one measure for slack while others use multiple measures. The same fact holds for the employed measures of performance. In the fifteen studies under investigation, the number of measures ranges from one single measure for each slack and performance (employed by e.g. Bradley *et al.*, 2011a and Latham and Braun, 2009) to a total amount of ten measures for slack and four measures for performance (employed by Tan and Peng, 2003).

Besides, when a performance metric is chosen, authors frequently fail to clearly state the applied definition of the specific metric (e.g. Chiu and Liaw, 2009; Latham and Braun, 2009). As mentioned before, e.g. for ROA several ways of calculation can be applied. Depending on the specific definition, the results of the performed analysis can vary strongly.

Greenley and Oktemgil (1998, p. 383) claim that not all measures of slack have an effect on all measures of performance. Therefore he recommends using multiple measures for both variables. On the other hand, the advantage of using a single measure is that the results are not biased due to the utilization of various, possibly overlapping categories of slack.

(3) Differences concerning the sample

Another factor that has to be considered when comparing the findings of the studies shown in Table 3 is that the sample characteristics, including sample size, firm characteristics, industries and periods of investigation, differ widely. The listed studies analyze samples ranging from survey data from 55 managers of state owned firms in the electronic industry to longitudinal financial data from 12.189 manufacturing firms over a 5 year period. Depending on the use of perceived or objective slack measures results can vary widely.

Also financial measures for slack cannot be generalized across industries, since the common amount of slack may differ widely from one industry to another (cf. Mousa, 2009, p. 78). In this regard, it is essential to control for industry. While eight of the listed studies are either concerned with firms from a single industry or use industry controls, others do not specifically control for industry effects. Besides, the location of the sample firms includes five US samples, four Chinese samples, two global samples as well as one Taiwanese, UK, Swedish and Belgium sample, which may result in regional differences.

(4) Differences concerning the context

Growing literature focuses on the environmental context, in which the slack-performance link is studied. Especially the influence of high uncertainty or threat in the environment, as well as scarcity of resources and opportunities is investigated. Specifically, six of the listed studies take the external environment into account. While some authors control for environmental munificence and dynamism (e.g. Bradley *et al.*, 2011a; Chiu and Liaw, 2009), others study the effects of slack during economic recession (e.g. Latham and Braun, 2009) or economic transition (e.g. Tan and Peng, 2003).

Latham and Braun (2009, p. 34) argue that in order to establish a better understanding of the effects and potential utilization of slack a more contextual approach is necessary. Bradley *et al.* (2011a, p. 1072) agrees that the effect of slack on performance varies strongly, depending on the favorability of the environment the firm is located in. Not least, since slack influences a firm's ability to respond to environmental changes, the environmental context plays an essential role in studying slack. The influence of the external environment on the relationship between slack and performance will be examined in more detail in section 3.3 Uncertainty and munificence in the external environment.

Despite the inconsistencies in previous literature and empirical evidence, the main findings of the reviewed studies as well as the results of Daniel *et al.'s* (2004, pp. 571–572) research show the tendency that particularly available slack has a positive effect on performance. However, it is crucial to note that moderators exist for all types of slack. Authors suggest that the environmental context (cf. Latham and Braun, 2009, p. 34), industry specific effects (cf. Mousa, 2009, p. 78) and organizational characteristics such as strategic orientation or ownership of firms (cf. Chiu and Liaw, 2009, p. 337; Ju and Zhao, 2009, p. 709) influence the effect of slack on performance. Therefore industry controls are essential when studying slack. Additionally, intervening variables on the relationship have to be investigated.

3.2.3 Intervening variables on the relationship

As pointed out by various authors (e.g. Daniel *et al.*, 2004, p. 572) it is crucial to take intervening variables on the relationship between slack and performance into account. Several authors focus on the effect of such intervening variables on the relationship. Proxies for strategic orientation (e.g. Chiu and Liaw, 2009), ownership level (e.g. Tan and Peng, 2003; George, 2005; Ju and Zhao, 2009), industry factors (e.g. Bradley et al., 2011a; Wefald et al., 2010b; Su et al., 2009) and external stakeholders (e.g. Vanacker et al., 2013) were employed as control variables and / or moderators. In addition, environmental factors have been found to influence slack and performance. Other prior studies examine the effect of slack on innovation, acquisitions and internationalization, environmental responsiveness, growth, and risk taking. These aspects influence the performance of a company and can therefore be viewed as intervening steps in the utilization of slack to enhance performance outcome (cf. Daniel *et al.*, 2004, p. 572; Mousa, 2009, p. 31). The findings of several authors on those topics have already been discussed in section 3.1.6 Potential utilization of slack, therefore only selected aspects, are restated and detailed here.

One function of slack, previously discussed in this thesis is that it facilitates strategic behavior. Since slack buffers organizations from downside risk, it encourages increased risk taking and enables companies to engage in more experimentation. This may lead to the introduction of new products, increased acquisition activities or internationalization (cf. Bourgeois, 1981, p. 31; Singh, 1986, p. 567; Lee, 2011, pp. 5–6). Thus the effect of slack on the performance of firms is influenced among other factors, by innovation and expansion strategies. In contrast to that, several authors additionally outline a potential negative effect of slack, as it promotes the generation of inefficiencies and suboptimal behavior. As excess resources are accumulated, a tendency towards self-serving decision making as well as undisciplined and irrationally optimistic behavior develops (cf. Chiu and Liaw, 2009, p. 323; Bourgeois, 1981, p. 31; Lin *et al.*, 2009, p. 399). This disadvantageous use of slack resources can be reduced by entrepreneurial orientation (cf. Heng and Xiuhao, 2010, p. 3).

Prior literature largely follows the notion that slack facilitates innovation. For instance, Nohria and Gulati (1996) state that slack resources are a major driver for innovation. Additionally, several authors highlight that the external environment is essential when studying slack in connection with innovation, as several environmental factors influence the innovation process (cf. Katila and Shane, 2005; Zona, 2012; Voss *et al.*, 2008). While slack can breed inefficiencies and therefore have a negative impact on innovation, particularly during times of crisis slack positively affects innovation. Due to environmental threat, managers tend to use resources more efficiently which mitigates the negative effect of slack. In addition, when slack resources are present managers are more willing to take risks resulting in increased innovation activities, such as product exploration (cf. Zona, 2012; Voss *et al.*, 2008, p. 160). Thus, firms can use slack resources to counter threats and invest in innovation, and thereby enable long term success which results in a positive effect on performance.

Regarding the impact of slack on the acquisition activities and expansion strategies of firms a similar picture is present. While lower levels of slack can inhibit internationalization due to irrational optimism and self-interested decisions of managers, especially high amounts of unabsorbed slack result in increased engagement in acquisition and activities and market expansion. A sufficient level of slack buffers a firm from the risk related to the acquisition and integration of another firm. Thus unabsorbed slack facilitates the search for new opportunities for change, resulting in more experimentation, acquisitions and increased internationalization activities (cf. Iyer and Miller, 2008; Lin *et al.*, 2009). Patzelt *et al.* (2008, p. 477) adds to the discussion that, when weaknesses within a company's capabilities exist, the presence of financial slack drives the search for the formation of new strategic alliances. Similarly, in a threatening and resource scarce external environment unabsorbed slack becomes especially beneficial. When environmental threat is present the potential negative impact of slack on efficiency and discipline diminishes, and scarce slack resources become a crucial factor for acquisitions and performance (cf. Wan and Yiu, 2009). Hence, unabsorbed slack is a major driver for acquisitions which leads to improved performance during crisis.

Mousa (2009) and Mousa and Reed (2013) investigate the impact of slack on success relating to new ventures. The authors note that the process of undergoing an IPO leads to increased uncertainty, greater managerial complexity and liability of newness. In this context, the availability of excess resources is crucial for a firm's success since it creates a competitive advantage. Particularly financial slack eases capital restrictions and thereby enables experimentation and increased risk taking, resulting in a positive effect on performance. Additionally slack provides flexibility, allowing managers to exploit emergent opportunities with positive performance implications and increase the rate of growth. The results of the authors show that when firms undergo an IPO, financial slack is highly valued by investors in the short term and increases the firm's chances of survival in the long run.

Overall the main findings of the above mentioned studies suggest that certain types of slack positively influence risk taking behavior, innovation activities, IPO success, and acquisition and internationalization strategies. It seems vital to take those aspects into account when studying the slack-performance link, since those factors intervene in the effect of slack on performance. Among others, Nohria and Gulati (1996, p. 1260) and Daniel *et al.* (2004, p. 572) suggest further research in this field. Hence, in the empirical part of this thesis, new product innovations, M&A activities and IPO deals are included as intervening variables.

3.3 Uncertainty and munificence in the external environment

As already broached in the previous chapter 3.2 The relationship between slack and performance has been studied in various contexts by previous authors. When reviewing the literature, it becomes clear that the external environment has substantial influence on the relationship. Sigerstad (2004, p. 53) states that the environment and its characteristics were implicit in the theory of slack from the very beginning, although environmental aspects were often neglected in subsequent literature. However, several recent authors note, that especially turbulences in the environment affect the influence slack has (e.g. Bradley *et al.*, 2011a, p. 1074; Chiu and Liaw, 2009, p. 329). Correspondingly, findings concerning the impact of uncertainty and munificence in the external environment will be discussed in more detail in this section of the literature review.

3.3.1 Definition of uncertainty and munificence

The external environment of a firm can be viewed as a source of information as well as a pool of resources. Hence, the dimensions of uncertainty (regarding information) and munificence (regarding resources) are some of the most fundamental characteristics of environments (cf. Sigerstad, 2004, p. 48; Bradley *et al.*, 2011a, p. 1074). Uncertainty is an inherent aspect of every company's business since a company's operations run over time and future events are unknowable. Especially certain entrepreneurial actions, such as the development of new products or services and the formation of new ventures, increase uncertainty (cf. McMullen and Shepherd, 2006, p. 133). Dependency on external resources additionally challenges firms as they make strategic decisions (cf. Bradley *et al.*, 2011a, p. 1074). Therefore coping with uncertainty and resource dependency by adapting to changing environments is essential for organizations in order to ensure long term survival.

(1) Environmental uncertainty

Uncertainty has been conceptualized in various ways in management, economics, as well as psychology literature (cf. McMullen and Shepherd, 2006, p. 133). In this thesis the term uncertainty will be defined according to Milliken (1987, p. 136), *as "individual's perceived inability to predict something accurately"*. In terms of environmental uncertainty, the unpredictability arises from the external environment of the organization, due to the lack of relevant data or the inability to distinguish between relevant and irrelevant information.

Duncan (1972, pp. 314–317) describes two dimensions of the environment which determine the degree of uncertainty: The dimension of complexity, determined by the number of factors in the environment, and the dimension of dynamism, referring to the rate of change of environmental factors. In conclusion, the author suggests that dynamic and complex environments possess the greatest degree of uncertainty. However, the dimension of dynamism has a stronger influence on uncertainty than complexity.

Milliken (1987, p. 135) notes that uncertainty can occur in three different forms. First, state uncertainty refers to the unpredictability of certain elements in the organizational environment. This is the case if future events are unpredictable or the probability or nature of changes is uncertain. Especially volatile, complex and heterogeneous environments are known to be less predictable. Second, effect uncertainty is the inability to predict the effect of environmental events on the organization itself. This includes the questions, if, how, when and how much an event will impact an organization. Third, response uncertainty occurs when individuals lack information about e.g. potential response options to environmental changes or the value and utility of the available choices, because the consequences of a response option are unknown. Effect and response uncertainty are increasingly salient, when environmental change (i.e. state uncertainty) is apparent and individuals perceive the need to act. In other words, individuals first become aware of response uncertainty, when environmental change occurs which the firm perceives as a threat or an opportunity (cf. Milliken, 1987, pp. 136–137; McMullen and Shepherd, 2006, p. 135).

In face of an economic downturn or crisis, the instability in the environment creates a lack of information about future events, the potential effect on firms as well as the outcome of decisions made in light of the crisis (cf. Bradley *et al.*, 2011a, p. 1075). Therefore the author of this thesis suggests that perceived state uncertainty is given, which leads to effect as well as response uncertainty among managers in firms. Consequently, in the next section no specific distinction between the three types of uncertainty is made.

(2) Environmental Munificence

Environmental munificence refers to the availability or scarcity of external resources that are required by firms sharing an environment. It affects the survival and growth possibilities of firms operating in the environment as well as the likelihood of new entrants (cf. Castrogiovanni, 1991, p. 542). When comparing it to slack as excess resources in the organization, munificence can be viewed as its environmental correlate, namely excess resources available from the environment (cf. Sigerstad, 2004, p. 45).

The main benefit of a highly munificent environment is that it facilitates survival. The more resources are available, the less external pressure is present. Additionally, high munificence is associated with increased opportunities by allowing greater diversity of goals, strategies, and organizational structures. However, highly munificent environments require fast decision making. Low munificence on the other hand, stands for environments where essential resources are scarce. Such a resource shortage in the environment leads to intense competition, diminishing strategic options, limited flexibility and fewer opportunities to gain competitive advantages. Since firms in resource scarce environments depend more on internal resources to develop opportunities, changes in organizational characteristics and the behavior of members are triggered when resources become limited (cf. Bradley *et al.*, 2011a, p. 1074; Castrogiovanni, 1991, p. 543; Koberg, 1987).

Previous literature on munificence highlights that it is crucial to define the level at which the environment is studied. The author of this thesis considers the macroeconomic level to be most appropriate. This level refers to the general demographic, economic, social, and political patterns and movements that have a significant influence on organizational characteristics and outputs (cf. Castrogiovanni, 1991, p. 546). When an environmental jolt occurs, the level of munificence in the macroeconomic environment usually changes dramatically. Due to the weakened munificence, resources become scarce, environmental opportunities limited, and the pressure among firms increases (cf. Wan and Yiu, 2009, p. 792).

Since uncertainty and munificence shape the external competitive environment of a firm, these factors influence the slack needs of a firm (cf. Bradley *et al.*, 2011a, p. 1074; George, 2005, p. 662). In addition, the ways firms utilize organizational slack are affected.

3.3.2 Impact of environmental uncertainty and munificence on slack

Before directly examining literature on the influence of the external environment on the slack-performance link, studies concerning effects of uncertainty, low munificence and environmental change on firms' resources are discussed. The review of those studies gives an insight on how uncertainty contributes to the accumulation of excess, slack resources.

(1) Impact of uncertainty and munificence on financial slack in the form of cash holdings

One way to hold financial slack within a firm is in the form of excess cash holdings. A large stream of literature is concerned with cash holdings and their development during environmental change due to financial constraints, economic downturn or crisis. In such a situation state uncertainty is generally high, since the environment is volatile. Hence, also effect and response uncertainty are likely to be increasingly perceived. Additionally, the fact that financial constraints are present implies that munificence is low. Thus, the financial resources available in the external environment are limited. However, the author wants to highlight at this point, that high cash holdings in a firm alone do not automatically translate into high levels of slack. Instead slack always constitutes an excess of liquid resources, thus additionally depends on the cash needs. Anyway high cash holdings indicate that financial slack is present in a firm.

Several studies on cash holdings provide support for the trade-off theory, stating that there is an optimum level of cash holdings, where the costs and benefits are ideally balanced. According to this theory, a firm can have four reasons to hold (excess) cash, namely transactional, precautionary, speculative, and taxation motives (cf. Ramírez and Tadesse, 2009, p. 388). Regarding the issue of financial slack in the context of uncertainty the precautionary motive for holding liquid assets is most significant, as it refers to the accumulation of excess cash as a cushion against unanticipated future events. This corresponds with the function of slack as a buffer from the external environment, as described in section 3.1.3 Role and functions of slack.

Empirical literature shows how certain firm specific variables influence the level of corporate cash holdings. First, the growth and investment opportunities of a firm drive its cash holdings. In addition cash flow volatility and other measures of risk, a high degree of information asymmetry as well as potentially high costs of financial distress contribute to the increase of cash holdings. Moreover, difficulties in financing due to the lack of access to capital markets were found to have an upward effect (cf. Opler *et al.*, 1999, p. 44; Ramezani, 2011, p. 1139; Ramírez and Tadesse, 2009, p. 388). Some of the mentioned factors such as unpredictability of cash flows and information asymmetry are typically intensified by external uncertainty. Others, such as the lack of excess to external capital are a form of resource dependence. Thus the empirical evidence on firm specific characteristics implies that uncertainty and resource scarcity in the environment induce firms to accumulate high cash holdings (i.e. financial slack).

Baum *et al.* (2004, pp. 4–5) agree that volatility in the macroeconomic conditions additionally affects a firm's level of liquid asset holdings. The authors argue that changes in the economic environment lead to increased uncertainty and an inability to accurately forecast future cash flows. Consequently managers are likely to consider a higher level of cash holdings appropriate. This suggestion was supported especially for large firms, firms experiencing rapid growth, financially constrained firms, and capital intensive firms.

Quite a few more studies investigate the implications of increased environmental uncertainty and resource scarcity such as an economic downturn on financially constrained firms. They find that constrained firms hold relatively higher cash positions which increase substantially when cash flow volatility is high, e.g. during economic depression (cf. Han and Qiu, 2007, p. 17; Pál and Ferrando, 2010, p. 30). Besides, such firms reduce technological and capital investments as well as employment to a greater extent. As a consequence of lacking external funding possibilities such firms tend to miss out on attractive investment opportunities (cf. Campello *et al.*, 2009, pp. 20–21). In addition, firms with higher debt dependence experience a greater decline in performance during crisis due to the high cost of additional debt capital (cf. Adjei, 2012, p. 184).

Ramírez and Tadesse (2009, p. 390) focus their study on corporate cash holdings in connection with the cultural factor uncertainty avoidance, and the multinationality of firms. They claim that the decision about the appropriate level of cash holdings as a precaution depends on the cultural factor of uncertainty avoidance. Countries, in which uncertainty is generally rather avoided, higher cash holdings are accumulated as a buffer against unanticipated future events. This is due to the fact that cash is the form of asset that can be deployed fast and for a variety of purposes.

(2) Impact of uncertainty and munificence on the relationship of slack and performance

The dimensions of uncertainty and munificence have been applied in a number of studies on organizational and especially available or unabsorbed slack. The suggested results however differ to some extent. Contrasting findings on slack and performance in dynamic, low munificent and complex environments are discussed here.

First, some authors find that the positive impact of slack on performance is stronger for dynamic and low munificent environments (e.g. Tan and Peng, 2003; Su *et al.*, 2009). Additionally, firms operating in an environment that is characterized by low munificence and high dynamism are confronted with increased competition on the market, resulting in higher complexity. Due to a high level of environmental uncertainty it becomes essential to develop new opportunities internally, e.g. through the introduction of new products. In order to sustain their competitive advantages, firms must engage in innovations which enhance performance. Furthermore, in such a dynamic environment, flexibility as well as strategic change and adaptation are a critical for survival and success. Moreover during economic transitions the financial market infrastructure is underdeveloped what makes it harder for firms to access resources externally. Since unabsorbed slack can be readily deployed for various purposes, it is highly valuable. The authors show a significant positive correlation between unabsorbed slack and firm performance in this hostile and uncertain environment (cf. Tan and Peng, 2003, p. 1253; Su *et al.*, 2009, pp. 76–80).

A possible explanation for this association is stated by Zona (2012, p. 44). The author highlights that uncertainty in the environment affects managers' risk attitude. Under conditions of unpredictable forecasts and potential losses, managers generally become more risk averse and reduce innovation investments. Slack resources counteract this behavior. As slack shields a firm from external risk and uncertainty to some extent, companies engage in more investment activities when slack is available, even in the face of high uncertainty. Similarly, Voss *et al.* (2008, p. 160) results show that under environmental threat, financial slack is positively associated with exploration rather than product exploitation. This suggests that companies use slack in order to counter threats and increase performance.

Others show that the positive relationship between slack and performance is stronger when munificence as well as dynamism is low. Bradley *et al.* (2011a, p. 1078) report that for new firms the slack–performance relationship is positive in low as well as highly dynamic environments, but strongest in environments with low dynamism and low munificence. The authors argue that in stable and resource scarce environments, new firms use internal resources such as slack to develop opportunities and thereby increase their performance, rather than rely on opportunities that are environmentally driven. However, the difference diminishes when higher levels of financial slack are present within the firm. Another interesting aspect of this study is the findings on the interaction effect between dynamism and munificence. While high munificence (i.e. high resource availability) generally leads to a negative effect of slack, in highly dynamic and uncertain environments slack has shown a positive effect, independent of resource availability. Thus, even in resource rich environments uncertainty leads to a positive association of financial slack with performance (cf. Bradley *et al.*, 2011a, p. 1087).

Finally, Latham and Braun (2009) reconcile arguments in favor of and against the positive impact of slack on performance during economic recession. The authors provide evidence that while higher levels of slack initially result in a steeper rate of decline, during economic recovery the presence of slack resources result in a faster rate of recovery. These results indicate that slack resources can be used as a cushion from external environmental turbulences. The utilization of slack resources for strategic activities during recession, allows for a more rapid recovery in the long term, providing those firms with an advantage in the post-recession period. Hence, the authors suggest that at the first signs of an economic recession slack resources should be hoarded for strategic use.

In summary it can be said that uncertainty in the environment generally leads to the accumulation of financial slack resources in the form of cash holdings. The results on the contingent and combined impact of environmental characteristics (uncertainty and munificence) on the slack-performance link are more mixed. Previous studies found evidence that in uncertain and highly dynamic environments financial slack leads to an increase in performance (cf. Tan and Peng, 2003, p. 1253), regardless of whether the environment is munificent or not. However, resource scarcity strengthens the effect of environmental uncertainty (cf. Bradley *et al.*, 2011a, p. 1087). Looking at the relationship of slack and performance over time, authors suggest that while slack initially has a decreasing effect on performance, during economic recovery slack resources can be used to speed up the rate of recovery (cf. Latham and Braun, 2009). Hence, the author of this thesis argues that uncertainty and low munificence lead to an increased positive effect of financial slack on performance.

3.3.3 The financial crisis as an example for high uncertainty and low munificence

In this thesis the term financial crisis refers to the global economic and financial market turmoil, triggered by the US subprime mortgage crisis in 2007. The crisis started with a US-wide decline in housing prices, causing a rise in subprime mortgage defaults in the beginning of 2007 (cf. Brunnermeier, 2008). In literature, excessive and risky lending practices in the US property market and a rapid expansion of complex financial products are stated as the main reasons for the outbreak of the crisis (cf. Johansson, 2011, p. 1088).

From the origin in the US subprime sector, the crisis spread through the US financial system and escalated globally. Soon the European financial sector was affected and exposed to sudden and severe increase in defaults. Struggling financial institutions started to reduce lending, what resulted in a credit crunch (cf. Campello *et al.*, 2009). The financial crisis spread through different channels, including financial sectors and real economy channels. Generally, it can be said that the financial turmoil had severe consequences for the real economy. In emerging as well as advanced countries sudden shortfalls in the export sectors weakened the economies, and firm values in various countries worldwide were affected (cf. Johansson, 2011).

A study, investigating the dynamic nature of regional financial market integration and regional volatility and correlations during the financial crisis shows a very strong increase in regional volatility in Europe during the financial crisis, especially after the Lehman Brothers bankruptcy on 15 September 2008. The authors show that Europe was severely affected during the global financial resulting in high volatility in the economic environment (cf. Johansson, 2011, pp. 1103–1104).

While the financial crisis is dramatic and unfortunate, it provides a unique opportunity to study how environmental turbulences, increased uncertainty and low munificence influence the relationship between slack and performance. Due to the financial turmoil and the rapid changes in the economy, high uncertainty in the firm's environment was created. As a result of the lack of information on future events managers were unable to accurately assess the effect the change might have on their organization. While in the beginning mainly financial institutions were affected, it remained unclear how the events would influence the real economy, resulting in managers' inability to accurately forecast future cash flow. In this regard it was difficult for firms to evaluate possible courses of action, since the outcome was unpredictable. In addition, the environmental jolt triggered by the financial crisis weakened the munificence in the environment substantially, resulting in limited externally available resources (e.g. financing, customer revenues, etc.). The credit crunch that resulted from the financial crisis, additionally lead to a lack of access to external capital, which added to the environmental uncertainty and resource scarcity.

3.4 Summary

The literature review shows that the concept of organizational slack is a frequently discussed topic and an important contribution to organizational science. Slack and its effects on an organization have been studied for several decades, since its first introduction into the literature in 1938 by Barnard (cf. Sigerstad, 2004, pp. 13–24). However, a multitude of partially contradictory or coinciding categorizations are applied and no broad agreement exists on the appropriate way of measurement for slack (cf. Krcal, 2012, pp. 683–685; Moses, 1992, p. 59).

The functions that slack fulfills are generally all based on the fundamental role of allowing room for maneuver. Specifically, slack acts as an inducement and a resource for conflict resolution, by offering the possibility to address a greater number of goals successively (cf. Bourgeois, 1981, p. 31). Besides, slack buffers a firm from the variations in the external environment. By absorbing conflicting external demands slack resources help a firm to survive and succeed especially in an uncontrollable external environment (cf. Chiu and Liaw, 2009, p. 323). Moreover slack resources facilitate certain strategic behavior as they increase a firm's ability to adapt to complex competitive landscapes, make modifications to its strategy and exploit external opportunities. Likewise, excess resources promote experimentation and risk taking within a firm (cf. Lin *et al.*, 2009, p. 398). On the contrary, slack can also negatively influence a company by inducing agency problems. As a result, undisciplined, inefficient, and irrationally optimistic behavior arises and the search for strategic options is conducted with less thoroughness and scrutiny (cf. Tan and Peng, 2003, p. 1251). A factor that can minimize such agency problems is the entrepreneurial orientation of a firm (cf. Heng and Xiuhao, 2010, p. 3).

Corresponding to the functions mentioned here, two basic views of slack are adopted in literature. In resource based and behavioral theory slack is viewed as a valuable resource for e.g. innovation, performance and growth. By agency theorists on the other hand, slack is described as inefficiency, resulting in a negative effect on the organization (cf. Lee, 2011, pp. 3–9). The empirical results of previous studies provide valuable insight on both perspectives. For instance certain types of organizational slack have been found to be a major driver for innovation (cf. Nohria and Gulati, 1996), to facilitate acquisitions and increased internationalization activities (cf. Iyer and Miller, 2008, p. 811), to induce risk taking (cf. Moses, 1992; Singh,

1986) and to boost as well as inhibit different methods of growth (cf. Bradley *et al.*, 2011b, pp. 548–549).

Concerning the effect of slack resources on performance, empirical evidence suggests that particularly unabsorbed types of slack have a positive influence on the performance of a firm (e.g. Lee, 2011; Bradley *et al.*, 2011a). However, authors point out that it is essential to apply industry controls and identify moderators when examining the association between slack and performance (cf. Daniel *et al.*, 2004, pp. 571–572). Additionally, studies highlight that a more contextual approach is necessary in order to accurately assess the relationship in different environmental settings (cf. Latham and Braun, 2009, p. 34).

Specifically uncertainty and munificence shape the environment of firms, and consequently influence organizational slack as well as its effect on performance. First, uncertainty and resource scarcity in the environment induce firms to accumulate financial slack in the form of cash holdings (cf. Baum *et al.*, 2004, pp. 4–5). Furthermore, prior studies suggest that uncertainty in the environment leads to a positive effect of financial slack on performance (cf. Tan and Peng, 2003, p. 1253). When external resources are limited the positive impact is strengthened further (cf. Bradley *et al.*, 2011a, p. 1087). Besides, authors found that in times of crisis or recession, slack initially results in a steeper rate of performance decline, but allows for a faster rate of recovery in the post-recession period (cf. Latham and Braun, 2009, p. 34).

Overall the concept of organizational slack is rather well established, thus the literature on organizational slack can be categorized as mature. On the other hand, studies on the relationship between slack and performance report partly inconsistent results. Particularly the context of environmental threat offers further room for research. Consequently the author categorizes the relevant theory for this thesis as intermediate.

4 Propositions and hypotheses

In this chapter the main findings of the literature review are combined and the propositions and hypotheses are formulated. Overall, this thesis focuses on the question whether the presence of financial slack influences corporate performance during times of crisis.

Previous studies partially found support for a positive relationship between financial slack and performance during environmental threat. However, it has been pointed out that additional research is necessary, since it is still unclear how intervening variables affect the relationship (c.f. Daniel *et al.*, 2004, p. 572). This study includes the investigation of three potentially intervening variables, namely the number of new products introduced, M&A completed, and IPO undergone. Moreover, since several authors highlight that controlling for industry is essential (e.g. Wefald *et al.*, 2010b, p. 71), the sample for this study has been drawn solely from the pharmaceutical industry. Besides, the context of the financial crisis is selected for this research, because recent studies highlight that a more contextual approach is necessary when examining organizational slack (e.g. Latham and Braun, 2009, p. 34). Specifically, the period between 2007 and 2010 reflects the environmental conditions of high uncertainty and low munificence.

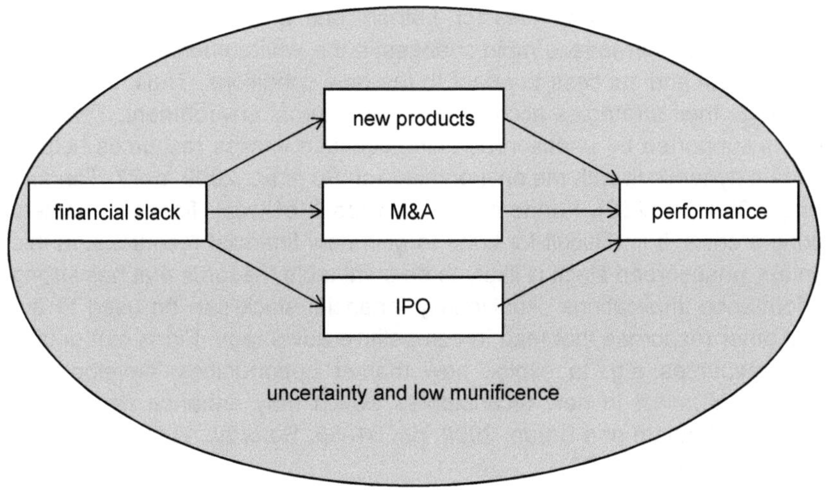

Figure 6: Conceptual model

The following conceptual model provides an overview on the variables included in this study. Financial slack is examined as the independent variable, and its effect on corporate performance as the dependent variable is studied in the context of environmental uncertainty and low munificence. In addition, three intervening variables are included, as shown in Figure 6.

4.1 Propositions and hypotheses concerning the impact of slack on performance

As shown in the investigation of recent studies on slack and performance, authors largely agree that slack, specifically in an available or unabsorbed form, has a positive influence on performance. For instance, Daniel *et al.* (2004) provide evidence on a positive influence of slack on performance. The authors argue that since available and potential slack are readily deployable and allow for high managerial discretion, those slack resources have a stronger influence on performance. Su *et al.* (2009, p. 77) and colleagues add that unabsorbed slack impacts performance more strongly in an uncertain environment.

The literature review revealed that slack can act as a buffer when a firm faces environmental threat. By deploying excess financial resources firms can maintain strategic investments and avoid staff reductions despite a possible decrease in revenues (cf. Latham and Braun, 2009, pp. 34–35). Moreover, when firms face rapid changes in the environment it is critical for their survival and success to adapt to the new conditions. Thus, they need to change their strategies according to the external environment. This process is supported by unabsorbed slack because excess resources help to create a dynamic fit with the environment (cf. Su *et al.*, 2009, p. 77; Tan and Peng, 2003, p. 1260). Furthermore, as a result of weak financial markets during a crisis, it is difficult for firms to gain new financial resources. In this context, unabsorbed slack is likely to be a valuable resource that has strong performance implications. Additionally, financial slack can be used to acquire other resources that lead to competitive advantage. Firms can deploy slack resources e.g. to exploit new market opportunities, develop new products or invest in new technologies, which may enhance firm performance (cf. Latham and Braun, 2009, pp. 34–35, Su *et al.*, 2009, p. 77; Tan and Peng, 2003, p. 1260).

A frequently criticized aspect of previous studies is the inconsistency in measurement of slack as well as performance (cf. Sigerstad, 2004, p. 44). Financial slack generally refers to excess liquid resources, not yet committed to specific organizational functions. This type of slack can be categorized as available, high discretion or unabsorbed slack, respectively. Concerning financial slack, the current ratio (=current assets divided by current liabilities) of a firm is widely adopted as a measure by previous authors (cf. Daniel *et al.*, 2004). Current assets are easily deployable and thus provide managers with high flexibility in resource allocation (cf. Su *et al.*, 2009, p. 81). Correspondingly, the current ratio captures available and unabsorbed forms of slack, since it represents the liquidity of a company (cf. Lee, 2011, p. 10).

Several studies of organizational slack emphasize that ROA is an appropriate measure for performance (cf. Lee, 2011, p. 10; Chiu and Liaw, 2009, p. 328). In this context, performance is defined as the profitability of an organization. However, various formulas for the calculation of the measure ROA exist in literature. Moreover, some authors use ROA as a performance metric, but do not state the exact definition applied (e.g. Latham and Braun, 2009; Chiu and Liaw, 2009; Greenley and Oktemgil, 1998). The standard definition of ROA is net income divided by total assets. Net income in this regard can include extraordinary P/L such as restructuring charges, unusual or nonrecurring items and results from discontinued operations. Besides, profit before tax instead of net income can be applied in order to cancel out any taxation differences as well as extraordinary P/L (cf. Krause and Arora, 2010, p. 41). Some authors focus on performance form an operating perspective, using EBITDA to calculate ROA (e.g. Love and Nohria, 2005; Ju and Zhao, 2009). In this definition, non-cash expenses such as depreciation and amortization are removed along with interest and taxes. It is essential to be aware of the fact that the specific choice of measure for performance can substantially influence the outcome of a study (cf. Sigerstad, 2004, p. 44).

From this the following propositions are made:

P_1: *Current ratio is a good indicator for financial slack.*

P_2: *Changes in the measurement of performance affect the relationship between financial slack and corporate performance.*

Given the arguments for the benefits of financial slack on performance in a highly uncertain environment, the author attempts to falsify the following null hypotheses:

$H0_1$: Financial slack (current ratio) has no influence on corporate performance measured as ROA_{EBITDA} during crisis.

$H0_2$: Financial slack (current ratio) has no influence on corporate performance measured as $ROA_{pre\text{-}tax}$ during crisis

$H0_3$: Financial slack (current ratio) has no influence on corporate performance measured as ROA_{ni} during crisis.

4.2 Propositions concerning intervening variables on the relationship

Prior authors point out that it is crucial to identify intervening variables on the relationship of slack and performance. For instance, strategic orientation, ownership level and the presence of venture capital or angel investors have shown to influence the relationship (cf. Chiu and Liaw, 2009; Ju and Zhao, 2009; Vanacker *et al.*, 2013). Besides, previous studies suggest that slack drives risk taking, innovation and expansion activities (cf. Nohria and Gulati, 1996; Voss *et al.*, 2008; Martinez and Kendall, 2006), which implies that those factors are likely to impact performance (cf. Mousa, 2009, p. 31). In this thesis, three specific intervening variables are suggested, namely M&A activities, the number of newly introduced products, and IPO.

Since slack buffers organizations from downside risk, it encourages increased risk taking and enables companies to engage in more experimentation, especially when external threat is present. As firms become more risk seeking, they increasingly use slack for innovation investments. Specifically unabsorbed slack has shown a positive correlation with product exploration under threat, suggesting that new product introductions can enhance performance (cf. Lee, 2011, pp. 5–6; Voss *et al.*, 2008, p. 160).

Additionally the buffering function of slack that promotes experimentation also encourages the engagement of a firm in market expansion, acquisitions and internationalization activities. Since slack resources increase the ability of a firm to adapt to complex competitive environments, they lead firms to explore opportunities in new markets and to expand globally (cf. Lin *et al.*, 2009, p. 399; Iyer and Miller, 2008, p. 811). Particularly during environmental jolts or when weaknesses within a company's capabilities exist, the presence of financial slack drives the search for acquisitions and the formation of new strategic alliances (cf. Patzelt *et al.*, 2008, p. 477; Wan and Yiu, 2009, p. 797), suggesting an increase of M&A activity which may enhance performance.

A third factor that may influence the relationship between slack and performance is the undergoing of an IPO. The transformation from a privately held to a public corporation increases a firm's vulnerability and entails greater managerial complexity and liability of newness. In the IPO period firms need more resources in order to absorb heightened costs and risks. Due to the unpredictability, a firm's financial resources become scarcer and thus more valuable, since they are crucial for continued existence and can lead to future competitive advantage (cf. Mousa, 2009; Mousa and Reed, 2013).

The preceding points support the following propositions:

P_3: *The introduction of new products influences the relationship between financial slack and corporate performance during crisis.*

P_4: *M&A activity influences the relationship between financial slack and corporate performance during crisis.*

P_5: *IPO influences the relationship between financial slack and corporate performance during crisis.*

5 Empirical results

In this chapter the results of the empirical analysis are presented. First the descriptive statistics and the results of the quantitative correlational analysis are explained. Thereafter, the results of the qualitative content analysis of the newspaper articles for the three moderating variables are presented.

5.1 Quantitative correlational analysis

In this study three definitions of ROA are used to measure performance: ROA using EBITDA, ROA using P/L before tax, and ROA using net income. The ROA_{EBITDA} of the sample ranges from 4.64% to 34.78%, whereof both extreme values are found in 2007. The lowest average ROA_{EBITDA} of all four years is found at Pelion SA with 5.89% and the highest is reported by Novo Nordisk A/S with 30.26%. The strongest fluctuations of the measure are present at Merck KGaA with a ROA of 33.03% in 2007 and values around 10% in the following years. No negative values or extreme outliers were identified for ROA_{EBITDA} in the investigation period.The highest average $ROA_{pre\text{-}tax}$ is reported by Novo Nordisk A/S with a maximum in 2010 at 29.78%. The performance values of the company are more than two standard deviations above the mean in 2008 to 2010. In 2009 the average $ROA_{pre\text{-}tax}$ of the whole sample was highest. The only negative values are reported in 2008 by Warner Chilcott with -0.45% and Akzo Nobel with -4.18%. In the same year the lowest average $ROA_{pre\text{-}tax}$ for the whole sample was reached.The maximum as well as minimum ROA_{ni} can be found at Akzo Nobel, in 2007 and 2008. However, the firm's extremely high ROA_{ni} of 48.49% in 2007 is a result of a non-recurring event. With a distance of approx. four standard deviations from the mean this value is an outlier. The year 2008 was the only year where ROA_{ni} was negative for any firm, with Akzo Nobel being the minimum with -5.8%. That year was also the year with the lowest average ROA_{ni} with 6.5% for the whole sample.

The current ratio of the sample firms ranges from minimum 0.475 in the year 2010 to maximum 5.412 in the year 2007. Meda AB is the firm with the lowest average current ratio of 0.714 in the whole period 2007 to 2010. The firm with the highest average current ratio for the whole period is Richter Gedeon Rt. with 4.835 on average, whereby the values for this firm have to be considered an outlier with a distance of approx. 3.8 standard deviations from the mean in the first three years. The average of all firms current ratio is lowest in the year 2008, where it amounts to 1.724. The highest fluctuations in current ratio are reported by Akzo Nobel NV, where the measure dropped from 3.38 in 2007 to below 1.5 in the following years.

The data from the mediator variables shows that most M&A as well as innovation activities took place in the years 2007 and 2009. In total 85 M&A activities were recorded in the entire investigation period. The highest numbers of acquisitions among the sample firms are 25 activities in 2009 and 22 activities in 2007. Regarding the introduction of new products, the picture is similar. Most of the 79 new product approvals were recorded in the years 2007 and 2009 with 26 new product approvals in each of these years. Besides, M&A as well as product innovation activities vary strongly among the sample firms. The firm with most M&A activities is Roche Holding AG reporting nine acquisitions, followed by Merck KGaA with eight and GlaxoSmithKline plc. with seven acquisitions. Three firms (Actelion ltd., Shire plc., and UCB SA), did not engage in any M&A activity during 2007 to 2010.

Most product approvals were achieved by Novartis AG, accounting for 22 approvals, followed by GlaxoSmithKline plc. with 18 new products. Further behind follow Sanofi with nine and Astrazeneca plc. as well as Merck KGaA with six new products each. For approximately half (twelve) of the sample firms no product introduction could be identified in the newspaper research. However, it has to be noted that only products approved (either in the US or EU) within the sample period were counted in this regard. Consequently firms may have products lacking formal approval or products rejected by the FDA or EMA in their portfolio which are not included in the analysis. Besides, only newspaper articles from selected sources were studied, thus product approvals not reported in those media were not identified.

Only two sample firms held an IPO during the investigation period. The Spanish pharmaceutical company Laboratorios Almirall SA (since July 2009 "Almirall SA") listed on the Madrid Stock Exchange in June 2007. Protek OAO, a Russian pharmaceuticals wholesaler started trading on the Moscow stock exchanges RTS and MISEX in April 2010. Due to the limited number of IPOs among the sample firms, their correlational results are insignificant.

Table 4 to Table 11 provide an overview of the correlations and descriptive statistics of the analyzed variables for each year between 2007 and 2010. The author chose to analyze the correlations on a year-to-year basis in order to examine how the variables and correlations changed during the crisis period. In addition, for the year 2010 a regression analysis was performed, as shown in Table 12.

Correlations

Year 2007		ROA_{EBITDA}	$ROA_{pre\text{-}tax}$	ROA_{ni}	Current ratio	Products	M&A	IPO
ROA_{EBITDA}	Pearson Correlation	1	.926**	.292	.153	.355	.521**	-.074
	Sig. (2-tailed)		.000	.157	.465	.081	.008	.725
	N	25	25	25	25	25	25	25
$ROA_{pre\text{-}tax}$	Pearson Correlation	.926**	1	.359	.182	.374	.547**	-.030
	Sig. (2-tailed)	.000		.078	.384	.066	.005	.889
	N	25	25	25	25	25	25	25
ROA_{ni}	Pearson Correlation	.292	.359	1	.432*	.243	.126	-.020
	Sig. (2-tailed)	.157	.078		.031	.242	.548	.924
	N	25	25	25	25	25	25	25
Current ratio	Pearson Correlation	.153	.182	.432*	1	-.102	.004	-.019
	Sig. (2-tailed)	.465	.384	.031		.628	.986	.928
	N	25	25	25	25	25	25	25
Products	Pearson Correlation	.355	.374	.243	-.102	1	.082	-.097
	Sig. (2-tailed)	.081	.066	.242	.628		.696	.644
	N	25	25	25	25	25	25	25
M&A	Pearson Correlation	.521**	.547**	.126	.004	.082	1	.200
	Sig. (2-tailed)	.008	.005	.548	.986	.696		.338
	N	25	25	25	25	25	25	25
IPO	Pearson Correlation	-.074	-.030	-.020	-.019	-.097	.200	1
	Sig. (2-tailed)	.725	.889	.924	.928	.644	.338	
	N	25	25	25	25	25	25	25

**. Correlation is significant at the 0.01 level (2-tailed).

*. Correlation is significant at the 0.05 level (2-tailed).

Table 4: Correlations for the year 2007

Descriptive Statistics

Year 2007	Mean	Std. Deviation	N
ROA_{EBITDA}	.147173	.0767724	25
$ROA_{pre\text{-}tax}$	.099956	.0720037	25
ROA_{ni}	.100727	.0988308	25
Current ratio	1.733664	.9783177	25
Products	1.04	2.226	25
M&A	.88	1.166	25
IPO	.04	.200	25

Table 5: Descriptive statistics for the year 2007

Table 4 shows that in the year 2007 independent variable current ratio and the dependent variable ROA_{ni} exhibit a moderate to strong positive relationship ($r=.432$), which is statistically significant ($p<.05$). The correlations between the other performance variables (ROA_{EBITDA} and $ROA_{pre\text{-}tax}$) and the slack variable however, are rather negligible and statistically insignificant.

The different performance measures themselves do not all show significant correlations with each other. Especially ROA_{ni} is merely weakly ($r<.36$) and insignificantly correlated to the other two ROA measures. The two measures ROA_{EBITDA} and $ROA_{pre\text{-}tax}$ on the other hand, have a very strong positive relationship with each other that is highly significant ($r=.926$ $p<.01$)

Regarding the intervening variables, there is a moderate positive correlation between performance and the introduction of new products ($r>.24$). This is true for all three measures of ROA in the year 2007. However, the correlation coefficient with ROA_{ni} is not significant, and also the results for the other two ROA definitions are only weakly significant ($p<0.1$).

For the variable IPO no strong or significant correlations were found. In this regard, it has to be noted that in the given sample not enough data exists for IPO activities. More specifically, only one IPO occurred during the year under investigation. Thus it is not possible to make any statement on the influence of the variable IPO based on this analysis.

The intervening variable which shows correlations that are highly significant at the 0.01 level is M&A. Specifically, M&A activities are strongly positive correlated with ROA_{EBITDA} ($r=.521$) and $ROA_{pre\text{-}tax}$ ($r=.547$). The correlation between M&A and ROA_{ni} is however negligible and not significant ($r=.126$ $p>.05$). The correlations among the moderating variables themselves are very low and not significant.

Correlations

Year 2008		ROA_{EBITDA}	$ROA_{pre\text{-}tax}$	ROA_{ni}	Current ratio	Products	M&A	IPO
ROA_{EBITDA}	Pearson Correlation	1	.839**	.795**	.261	.006	-.041	.b
	Sig. (2-tailed)		.000	.000	.208	.977	.845	.
	N	25	25	25	25	25	25	25
$ROA_{pre\text{-}tax}$	Pearson Correlation	.839**	1	.972**	.397*	.073	.014	.b
	Sig. (2-tailed)	.000		.000	.050	.730	.948	.
	N	25	25	25	25	25	25	25
ROA_{ni}	Pearson Correlation	.795**	.972**	1	.415*	.040	-.068	.b
	Sig. (2-tailed)	.000	.000		.039	.848	.745	.
	N	25	25	25	25	25	25	25
Current ratio	Pearson Correlation	.261	.397*	.415*	1	-.086	.265	.b
	Sig. (2-tailed)	.208	.050	.039		.683	.201	.
	N	25	25	25	25	25	25	25
Products	Pearson Correlation	.006	.073	.040	-.086	1	-.002	.b
	Sig. (2-tailed)	.977	.730	.848	.683		.991	.
	N	25	25	25	25	25	25	25
M&A	Pearson Correlation	-.041	.014	-.068	.265	-.002	1	.b
	Sig. (2-tailed)	.845	.948	.745	.201	.991		.
	N	25	25	25	25	25	25	25
IPO	Pearson Correlation	.b	.b	.b	.b	.b	.b	.b
	Sig. (2-tailed)	.	.	.	.	.	.	
	N	25	25	25	25	25	25	25

**. Correlation is significant at the 0.01 level (2-tailed).
*. Correlation is significant at the 0.05 level (2-tailed).
b. Cannot be computed because at least one of the variables is constant.

Table 6: Correlations for the year 2008

Descriptive Statistics

Year 2008	Mean	Std. Deviation	N
ROA_{EBITDA}	.154000	.0653197	25
$ROA_{pre\text{-}tax}$	.086800	.0719792	25
ROA_{ni}	.064800	.0590988	25
Current ratio	1.617200	.8560691	25
Products	.48	1.262	25
M&A	.84	1.143	25
IPO	.00	.000	25

Table 7: Descriptive statistics for the year 2008

Overall, the correlations table for the year 2008 (Table 6) shows stronger correlations between the independent and dependent variables, compared to the year before.

The current ratio has a moderate to strong positive correlation coefficient with ROA_{ni} (r=.415) as well as $ROA_{pre\text{-}tax}$ (r=.397), though the correlation is stronger for ROA_{ni}. Both correlations are significant at the 0.05 level. The performance metric ROA_{EBITDA} however is only weakly and statistically insignificantly correlated with current ratio (r=.261 p>.05).

In contrast to the previous year, in 2008 strong correlations among all performance metrics are present. All three measures of ROA are very strongly positively correlated (r > .79) and the correlation coefficients are highly significant (p<.01).

No statistically significant correlations are found for the intervening variables new products and M&A activities. All correlation coefficients in this regard are negligible. For IPO no values are calculated for the year 2008, since none of the sample firms underwent an IPO in this period.

Correlations

Year 2009		ROA_{EBITDA}	$ROA_{pre-tax}$	ROA_{ni}	Current ratio	Products	M&A	IPO
ROA_{EBITDA}	Pearson Correlation	1	.947**	.895**	.251	.225	-.066	.b
	Sig. (2-tailed)		.000	.000	.227	.280	.755	.
	N	25	25	25	25	25	25	25
$ROA_{pre-tax}$	Pearson Correlation	.947**	1	.978**	.272	.271	-.086	.b
	Sig. (2-tailed)	.000		.000	.189	.190	.684	.
	N	25	25	25	25	25	25	25
ROA_{ni}	Pearson Correlation	.895**	.978**	1	.328	.269	-.084	.b
	Sig. (2-tailed)	.000	.000		.109	.194	.691	.
	N	25	25	25	25	25	25	25
Current ratio	Pearson Correlation	.251	.272	.328	1	-.081	-.256	.b
	Sig. (2-tailed)	.227	.189	.109		.701	.216	.
	N	25	25	25	25	25	25	25
Products	Pearson Correlation	.225	.271	.269	-.081	1	.360	.b
	Sig. (2-tailed)	.280	.190	.194	.701		.077	.
	N	25	25	25	25	25	25	25
M&A	Pearson Correlation	-.066	-.086	-.084	-.256	.360	1	.b
	Sig. (2-tailed)	.755	.684	.691	.216	.077		.
	N	25	25	25	25	25	25	25
IPO	Pearson Correlation	.b	.b	.b	.b	.b	.b	.b
	Sig. (2-tailed)	.	.	.	.	.	.	
	N	25	25	25	25	25	25	25

**. Correlation is significant at the 0.01 level (2-tailed).
b. Cannot be computed because at least one of the variables is constant.

Table 8: Correlations for the year 2009

Descriptive Statistics

Year 2009	Mean	Std. Deviation	N
ROA_{EBITDA}	.154000	.0623164	25
$ROA_{pre-tax}$	.103600	.0587991	25
ROA_{ni}	.081600	.0452475	25
Current ratio	1.724400	.8946744	25
Products	1.04	2.189	25
M&A	1.00	1.323	25
IPO	.00	.000	25

Table 9: Descriptive statistics for the year 2009

In the year 2009 the results of the analysis from Table 8 shows no statistically significant correlations between the variable for financial slack and any of the three performance metrics. While the correlation coefficients vary between .251 for ROA_{EBITDA} and .328 for ROA_{ni}, thus implying a weak to moderate positive correlation, the significance for all variables remains above the 0.05 level.

Just as in the year 2008, the three performance metrics ROA_{EBITDA}, $ROA_{pre-tax}$ and ROA_{ni} have a very strong positive and statistically significant correlation among each other ($r>.89$ $p<.01$).

Concerning the intervening variables the correlation coefficient of -.256 between M&A activities and financial slack suggests a weak negative relationship between the variables. However, the result is not statistically significant ($p>.05$). In fact, the intervening variables new products and M&A are not significantly correlated with any of the other variables. Again, for IPO no values are calculated for the year 2009, since none of the sample firms underwent an IPO in this period.

Correlations

Year 2010		ROA_{EBITDA}	$ROA_{pre-tax}$	ROA_{ni}	Current ratio	Products	M&A	IPO
ROA_{EBITDA}	Pearson Correlation	1	.893**	.763**	.091	.080	-.178	-.275
	Sig. (2-tailed)		.000	.000	.665	.703	.394	.183
	N	25	25	25	25	25	25	25
$ROA_{pre-tax}$	Pearson Correlation	.893**	1	.877**	.178	.105	-.066	-.182
	Sig. (2-tailed)	.000		.000	.396	.617	.754	.384
	N	25	25	25	25	25	25	25
ROA_{ni}	Pearson Correlation	.763**	.877**	1	.473*	.028	-.130	-.224
	Sig. (2-tailed)	.000	.000		.017	.894	.535	.282
	N	25	25	25	25	25	25	25
Current ratio	Pearson Correlation	.091	.178	.473*	1	-.180	.017	-.135
	Sig. (2-tailed)	.665	.396	.017		.389	.935	.520
	N	25	25	25	25	25	25	25
Products	Pearson Correlation	.080	.105	.028	-.180	1	.034	-.131
	Sig. (2-tailed)	.703	.617	.894	.389		.873	.534
	N	25	25	25	25	25	25	25
M&A	Pearson Correlation	-.178	-.066	-.130	.017	.034	1	.672**
	Sig. (2-tailed)	.394	.754	.535	.935	.873		.000
	N	25	25	25	25	25	25	25
IPO	Pearson Correlation	-.275	-.182	-.224	-.135	-.131	.672**	1
	Sig. (2-tailed)	.183	.384	.282	.520	.534	.000	
	N	25	25	25	25	25	25	25

**. Correlation is significant at the 0.01 level (2-tailed).
*. Correlation is significant at the 0.05 level (2-tailed).

Table 10: Correlations for the year 2010

Descriptive Statistics

Year 2010	Mean	Std. Deviation	N
ROA_{EBITDA}	.148800	.0748510	25
$ROA_{pre\text{-}tax}$	.090800	.0696372	25
ROA_{ni}	.076400	.0525103	25
Current ratio	1.752800	.8075195	25
Products	.60	.957	25
M&A	.68	1.030	25
IPO	.04	.200	25

Table 11: Descriptive statistics for the year 2010

Table 10 presents the correlation results of the year 2010, where the independent variable for financial slack and the dependent variable ROA_{ni} are rather strongly positively correlated (r=.473) at a 0.05 level of significance. ROA_{EBITDA} as well as $ROA_{pre\text{-}tax}$ however do not exhibit a correlation with current ratio.

The correlations among the three performance metrics are strongly positive (r>.76) and highly significant (p<.01), as already demonstrated in the years 2008 and 2009.

The correlation table for the year 2010 also shows that M&A and IPO activities are strongly positively correlated (r=.672), at a highly significant level (p<.01). However it has to be highlighted here once more that not enough data exists for IPO activities in the given sample in order to make a statement about the influence of the variable. Only one firm underwent an IPO during the year under investigation. Beside this result, no statistically significant correlations were identified for the intervening variables.

For the significant correlation result of current ratio and ROA_{ni} a regression analysis was performed, as presented in Table 12.

The regression model 1 contains the independent variable current ratio and the dependent variable ROA using net income. The F-statistic value indicates the overall significance of the model, while the R^2 statistic value indicates how good the independent variable is at predicting the dependent variable. The model is significant with R^2=.224 and adjusted R^2=.190 at p<.05 (F=6.621). Thus, approx. 22% of the deviation of ROA_{ni} can be explained by its relationship to current ratio.

Model Summary[b]

Model	R	R Square	Adjusted R Square	Std. Error of the Estimate
1	.473[a]	.224	.190	.0472658

a. Predictors: (Constant), Current ratio
b. Dependent Variable: ROA_{ni}

ANOVA[a]

Model		Sum of Squares	df	Mean Square	F	Sig.
1	Regression	.015	1	.015	6.621	.017[b]
	Residual	.051	23	.002		
	Total	.066	24			

a. Dependent Variable: ROA_{ni}
b. Predictors: (Constant), Current ratio

Coefficients[a]

Model		Unstandardized Coefficients		Standardized Coefficients	t	Sig.
		B	Std. Error	Beta		
1	(Constant)	.023	.023		.980	.337
	Current ratio	.031	.012	.473	2.573	.017

a. Dependent Variable: ROA_{ni}

Table 12: Regression analysis for the year 2010

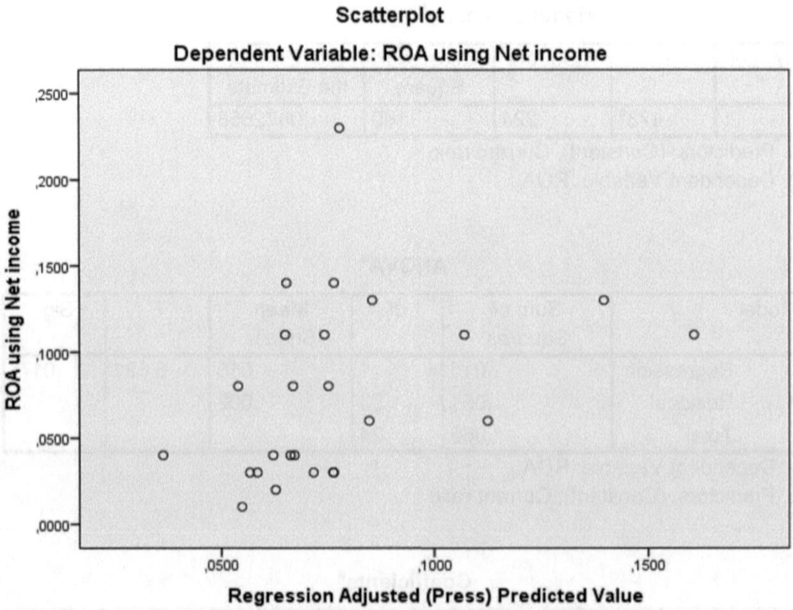

Figure 7: Scatterplot for regression analysis for the year 2010

5.2 Qualitative content analysis

The newspaper research showed that the main challenges for pharmaceutical firms during the investigation period were a heightened level of competitiveness among firms, expiring patent protections for big selling drugs and regulatory pressures combined with the negative impact of the financial crisis on the economic environment.

The heightened level of competitiveness in the industry is reflected e.g. by the increased number of generic drug approvals. The use of generics dramatically increased in the period under investigation. This trend was intensified as blockbuster drugs lost patent protection and healthcare costs rose. While patent protected drugs are highly profitable, patent expirations allow generics to offer comparable products at much lower prices. Traditional strategies for restoring sales, such as launching an improved product became less effective. Since insurers and governments became increasingly cost conscious, a significant benefit over cheaper generics was necessary to achieve a higher price.

One key challenge for new product introductions is the governmental approval. Delays in a drug approval process have significant consequences for pharmaceutical firms. For example, if rival products are able to establish their lead on the market, it becomes more difficult for the delayed product to penetrate the market once it is approved. Due to heightened scrutiny, the FDA required larger studies of new drugs, resulting in increasing R&D costs for the pharmaceutical firms. The FDA negated the criticism and claimed that the number of approvals had declined because companies were submitting fewer drugs for approval. The approval standards concerning safety and efficiency for new drug applications however had not changed.

Concerning pharmaceutical firms' innovation and acquisition strategies, targeted acquisitions, alliances and licensing deals were commonly used. Firms acquired small and medium-sized companies to strengthen their main business. The M&A markets in the investigation period were strongly influenced by the financial crisis. For instance, in the first three quarters of 2008, the global deal volume was down 23%. The turmoil on the credit and stock markets generally made it more difficult for companies to finance deals and to agree on an appropriate price. While some firms rather avoided big M&A activities due to high uncertainty, firms with sufficient financial resources were able to take advantage of the weak equity markets and declining valuations of companies to make cheap acquisitions.

5.2.1 Novartis AG – most new products

The highest number of new product approvals between 2007 and 2010, namely 22 new products was reported for Novartis. Novartis is one of the biggest pharmaceutical companies in the world. In the beginning of 2007 it was on the third rank in the industry worldwide. The company's growth strategy involves organic growth and acquisitions. The growth drivers in the core pharmaceutical business at the beginning of the investigation period were the drugs Diovan (high blood-pressure) and Glivec (leukemia). Comparing the current ratio of the sample firms, Novartis reported a figure below average in all periods under investigation, except in 2009. The R&D expenses of the firm as a percentage of sales ranged between 16% and 17.5% during the investigation period, which was slightly above average in the industry.

Reported results of Novartis during the investigation period

For the year 2007 Novartis planned a record of eight new product launches on the US market alone. In the first half of the year, Novartis could maintain its good performance and reported sales and profit ahead of market expectations. Especially the generics unit Sandoz and the recently acquired vaccines and diagnostics unit improved sales. The cash holdings of the company increased during this time. In the course of the year Novartis encountered severe competition from generic products and hit some regulatory difficulties. In addition the removal of one of its drugs from the US market lowered sales. As a result, two key positions in the pharmaceutical business of the company were replaced, namely the head of pharmaceuticals and head of pharmaceuticals marketing. Besides, over 1000 jobs in US sales and marketing were cut. By the end of 2007 the company reported a 45% drop in its fourth quarter net profit, due to the restructuring charge for its cost savings program. Under this program the company closed research centers and cut 2,500 jobs worldwide. In comparison to the sample peer group Novartis' performance measured in ROA_{EBITDA} was below average. However, measured in ROA_{ni} Novartis was among the top 5 performing companies.

In 2008 Novartis reported a profit growth. The financial crisis affected consumer behavior, which way why sales of non-prescription medicines fell in 2008 as consumers preferred less expensive, generic products. Sales of branded prescription drugs rose slightly, while the sale of generics was disappointing due to problems at a generics factory in the US and the lack of new products. Novartis stated that instead of focusing on acquisition, the firm wants to grow organically and invest into innovation through R&D. In comparison to the sample peer group of this study, Novartis increased its ROA_{EBITDA}. The company's ROA_{ni} remained above average.

In the year 2009 new products and the firm's innovative influenza vaccine lead to strong sales and earnings. In addition, higher productivity and cost improvement measures increased the net profit significantly. Overall Novartis demonstrated a strong market position, despite continuing budget constraints as well as price erosions in Europe's economy. However, its ROA_{EBITDA} was below average, compared to the other sample firms. The current ratio of the firm was slightly above average.

In 2010 Novartis net profits and sales were improved. The approval of the new Gilenya drug for multiple sclerosis, strong demand for the new generic version of a blood thinner and the cancer drug blockbuster Afinitor lead to increased performance. In total, recently introduced products made up more than 20% of Novartis's revenues, with the diabetes drug Galvus and the blood-pressure drug Tekturna being the main growth drivers in Novartis pharmaceutical business. The consolidation of the recently acquired eyecare company Alcon further boosted sales. However, price cuts and the US healthcare reform weakened the firm's growth. ROA_{ni} and $ROA_{pre\text{-}tax}$ of Novartis were above average. The current ratio was among the low quartile of the sample firms, implying very high operating efficiency.

Strategy of Novartis and performance influencing aspects

One competitive advantage of Novartis is the combination of its business operations in innovative as well as generic pharmaceuticals. While the core pharmaceutical business of Novartis invests heavily in R&D to discover and develop new medicines, its Sandoz subsidiary is the world's second biggest generics unit. This constitutes to the firms rich drug portfolio.

During the investigation period a big challenge for Novartis was the risk of patent exposure for its well-established bestseller drugs Diovan and Gleevec, accounting for approx. 20% of the company's sales. While these drugs were highly profitable due to patents, patent expirations allow generics to offer comparable products at much lower prices. Novartis' strategy to cope with the patent expiration and to secure new sales growth is a multifaceted approach, including investments in new drugs for cancer and other diseases as well as aggressive expansion in emerging markets. Accordingly, Novartis boosted spending on clinical trials, and tested some drugs simultaneously on several different diseases. The company increased diversification e.g. in the fields of diagnostics, vaccines and other healthcare, achieved partly through selective acquisitions and the building of a new vaccine plant in the US in 2009. Moreover, Novartis intensified its engagement in emerging markets with good growth prospects, such as Russia, China and Brazil.

During the financial crisis Novartis focused increasingly on efficiency, productivity and cost-cutting measures. As pharmaceutical firms faced challenges in their environment, the existing size and cost structure could not be sustained. Hence, reorganization including slimmer and more flexible cost structures and new leaders was necessary for many firms to stay successful. By cutting sales and marketing spending, streamlining procurement and making better use of manufacturing facilities, Novartis managed to overcome the threat imposed by the financial crisis.

While in the past, Novartis and most other pharmaceutical firms focused on treatments for common diseases that offered a large number of potential patients, Novartis increasingly engages in the development of drugs for rare diseases, where few treatments are known. Starting in 2002 Novartis invested heavily in genetics-focused research, which concentrates on the investigation of genetic triggers that cause disease. As a result of this effort, the drug Ilaris was approved in 2009. The product treats a rare genetic disorder affecting only a few thousand people worldwide. Novartis continued testing the drug on a more common condition with similar causes, attempting to expand the drugs' use other diseases with similar genetic triggers.

Besides, Novartis increased its investments in cancer research since this segment was highly profitable and experienced strong sales growth. The leukemia treatment Gleevec became Novartis's second best selling product in 2007, and the company planned to start selling several new cancer drugs in the following years. In accordance with this strategic focus, Novartis made an acquisition in 2009 to expand into generic cancer drugs. This effort helped to broaden the portfolio of Novartis's Sandoz subsidiary.

Another key aspect of Novartis growth strategy was the investment in generic versions of biotech drugs, developed at the Sandoz subsidiary. Due to the high complexity of biotech drugs and the more recent filing dates of their patents, the biotechnology industry had previously operated without the threat of lower priced generic products. Sandoz was one of the pioneers in generic biological medicines and had several products filed for approval in Europe. The fast growing market for biological medicines was highly attractive for generics since innovative drugs in this sector were extremely expensive. As a generic manufacturer, Sandoz was able to offer the product 25-30 % cheaper than the original medicine. However, the equivalence of generic biotech drugs was more difficult to assess. Thus the penetration of the market posed some difficulties.

Next to the development of new products, acquisitions are closely related to innovative activities. Novartis performed a few selective acquisitions in the period under investigation, in order to diversify in different segments of healthcare, strengthen its portfolio and insulate itself from the effect of the impending loss of patent protection. However, the company focused more on organic growth and the investment in R&D instead of intensive M&A activities. Novartis R&D expenditure as a percentage of sales was above average compared to its industry competitors. The emphasis on in-house R&D is one of Novartis' strategic focuses.

Novartis finely managed its research portfolio in order to maintain a strong pipeline of future drugs. This includes the discontinuation of studies on less promising medicines. In 2010 Novartis discontinued the development of a few compounds in favor of developing other treatments with better prospects. However, the decision to close the research on a drug can turn out to be a mistake. For instance, in the 1990s Novartis was researching in the field of heart disease, but gave up because the product was too expensive to manufacture profitably. A Novartis executive received the permission to license the development rights and founded a business in 1998, which Novartis invested in. This company worked on simplifying the drug's chemical synthesis. Novartis reserved the right to buy the drug back, which it did in 2002 after the research showed first positive results. Finally, in 2009 Novartis fully acquired the company and integrated the research back into its business. The product, marketed under the name Tekturna became one of Novartis best-seller products in 2010. This incident highlights the intense pressure that big pharmaceutical firms face to make profits. Consequently they are skeptical of long shots, funding research into only the most promising projects.

5.2.2 Roche Holding AG – most M&A activities

The firm with most acquisitions between 2007 and 2010 was Roche, counting 9 M&A activities. Roche is a family controlled pharmaceutical company, which focuses on pharmaceuticals and diagnostics. Measured by market value, Roche was Europe's largest pharmaceutical company in the beginning of the investigation period. The firm was one of the best performing companies in the industry, with cash flow boosted by strong revenues from its portfolio of cancer treatments. Due to the share structure, it is more difficult for Roche to raise money in the capital markets, compared to some rivals. Correspondingly, the firm continuously held high cash resources to allow maximum flexibility for acquisitions. The R&D spending of the firm as a percentage of sales increased steadily during the examined years, from 18.2% in 2007 to 21.1% in 2010, and was well above average in the industry.

Reported results of Roche during the investigation period

In 2007 Roche achieved strong performance, with increases in sales as well as net income. While other big pharmaceutical firms presented results below expectations, Roche was able to accomplish growth ahead of the industry. Around 20% of Roche's sales were achieved in diagnostics, while 80% of sales resulted from prescription drugs. The main growth drivers were its new cancer drugs Avastin and Herceptin, developed by Genetech a majority owned, independent subsidiary of Roche. In addition, the demand for the influenza drug Tamiflu rose strongly in the first half of the year, since governments stockpiled the drug in case of an influenza outbreak. The diagnostics market grew slowly, but was boosted by acquisitions. Roche's ROA was among the top 25% of the sample firms. Also the firm's current ratio was among the highest ones.

In the year 2008 Roche had to deal with slowing sales growth, which resulted in a decrease of net income of 5%. To a large extent, the sales decline was caused by a drop of demand for Tamilfu (-71% in the first quarter), since governments had already built up large reserves of the influenza treatment. The cancer drugs MabThera, Herceptin and Avastin were Roche's top sellers, with sales rising by 15%. In the diagnostics division, operating profit fell due to amortization of and investments in recently acquired companies, as well as fierce competition in the US diabetes market. In July 2008, Roche announced its plan to fully take over the majority owned but independent subsidiary Genetech. In comparison to the sample, Roche maintained its high ROA and current ratio.

The performance of Roche in 2009 was weakened by one-offs relating to the acquisition of Genetech, which led to an overall decline in net income. Integration costs for the acquired firm resulted from the building stop of a new plant at Genentech's main site, the closing of manufacturing operations at Roche's former US headquarters and the closing of an R&D center. Sales in core pharmaceutical grew twice as fast as their market, partly due to expanded use of some of the top selling drugs. In addition, sales of Tamiflu grew again due to the threat of a swine flu pandemic. In the diagnostics division sales grew slightly. Roche's ROA_{ni} as well as its current ratio fell compared to the sample peer group, but both remained above average.

In 2010 Roche reported strong performance again. Net profit increased despite high costs for the firm's restructuring program. The pharmaceutical sales of the firm grew well in the first three quarters of the year, driven by sales growth of cancer treatments which accounted for almost half of Roche's sales. However, in the last quarter sales were weakened due to the US healthcare reform and price cuts in Europe. Regarding the integration of Genetech, first cost savings were achieved. Due to strong cash flows, Roche was able to repay one third of the debt taken on for the Genentech deal by the end of 2010. ROA as well as current ratio of Roche were above average.

Strategy of Roche and performance influencing aspects

Roche's strategic focus lies in the combination of its pharmaceuticals and diagnostics businesses. This twin-pillar strategy gives Roche a competitive advantage over its rivals, since diagnostics help to better target therapies to patients and thus cut the costs and risks of developing new drugs. Since Roche has an internal diagnostics division it does not rely on external partners in this regard and thus is in full control, which contributes to well managed overall R&D expenditure. While most of Roche's competitors follow a more diversified approach to spread the risk over more divisions Roche has a rather narrow strategic focus.

Roche moved aggressively to build its diagnostics business in the investigation period. The company beliefs that machines and other tools that help diagnose and monitor disease will be crucial in developing medicines in the future. Following this approach, Roche heavily invested in this field and acquired several diagnostic firms in the US. Among them, Ventana Medical Systems Inc. which tests tissue to diagnose women with a genetically determined form of breast cancer. Roche's drug Herceptin targets this kind of cancer, which offers potential synergies and opportunities to develop drugs that target the underlying cause of a disease more accurately. To further enhance the interaction between pharmaceuticals and diagnostics within the company, Roche appointed its former head of diagnostics as new CEO in March 2008.

Concerning prescription drug sales Roche was better placed than most of its rivals, mainly because of its portfolio of specialty medicines. Most of Roche's income resulted from hospital prescribed biological treatments like Avastin, which have wide applications in cancer and had been relatively shielded from generic competition. Drugs to come off patent between 2008 and 2012 accounted for only 11 % of Roche's sales in 2007, while the industry average was at approx. 29%. By specializing in cancer treatments Roche focused on small groups of patients with life threatening disease, thus minimizing the pricing pressure and avoiding the need for costly large primary care sales forces. Due to strong cash flows Roche was able to finance substantial acquisitions in the investigation period, which helped to further strengthen its drug portfolio.

In 2008 Roche acquired a closely held UK biotechnology firm, which allowed it access to a new way of treating cancer. Besides, it bought a Canadian biotech firm to further develop the cancer and immunology business as well as a US firm to expand in gene therapy. Roche raised its stake in Chugai, a leading Japanese biotechnology firm which had been in a strategic alliance with Roche since October 2002. Roche had a very strong financial position thus it did not experience severe financial problems during the crisis. Correspondingly, the firm was able to take advantage of the weak equity markets and declining valuations of companies to make several acquisitions as potential targets became cheaper.

A topic that was very present in the media was Roche's acquisition of Genetech, the world's second biggest biotechnology company by sales. The controlling stake of Genetech was sold to Roche in the 1990, despite independency concerns to ensure financial stability. Similarly to the case of Chugai, Roche initially decided that continuing arms-length management was the best way to preserve innovative R&D and encourage the biotech company's entrepreneurial spirit. Roche changed its strategy when it decided to acquire the remaining 44% stake of Genetech in July 2008. When Genetech did not agree to a takeover at the offered price, Roche turned hostile, but later increased its offer again and finally agreed on an acquisition in March 2009. Despite the financial crisis Roche was able to raise enough cash for the mega merger, due to high liquidity, an equity ratio of approx. 70% and its high credit worthiness. A record $30 billion was raised in the US and European corporate bond markets to help finance the offer. The combined dollar, euro and sterling note offer was the biggest corporate debt financing since early 2000. The rest of the capital needed came from banks. Due to increased debt after the deal Fitch Ratings cut Roche's credit rating to AA and outlook to negative from stable.

One crucial factor in the change of strategy was the growing dependence of Roche on Genetech. In 2007, around two thirds of Roche's pharmaceutical sales were achieved with products developed by Genetech. Besides, according to an agreement from 1999 Roche's right to license and sell Genentech drugs outside of the US expired in 2015, thus a potentially complicated renegotiation was avoided by the full acquisition. Through the takeover Roche gained full control of all the revenues of Genetech's drugs and access to the attractive portfolio of new medicines under development. By merging many of the companies' operations, Roche achieved economies of scale in R&D and marketing and simplified the structure of the combined entity, thus allowing annual cost savings, improved information flows and closer cooperation. However, Roche risked upsetting the highly successful but delicate relationship the partners had developed. Since the corporate cultures of the two companies were extremely different, it was unclear if Genentech's culture, encouraging creativity, entrepreneurialism and innovation, could survive under Roche's full control. Thus, the challenge for Roche for a successful integration was retaining employees and preserving the company's culture. To enable successful integration and synergies Roche made Genentech the US headquarters of the combined company. Marketing policies became more consistent and manufacturing and administrative duplication was eliminated through restructuring and job cuts. While the early-stage drug research continued to run as an independent group within Roche, the research groups carrying out late-stage human trials of medicines were combined. The Genentech takeover transformed Roche into a pharma-biotech organization to ensure earnings growth in the short term through synergies, and in the long term through high R&D innovation. In addition, the deal reinforced and recentralized the focus of the group on specialty care medicines and diagnostics. Further deals to extend its dominant position in cancer diagnostics followed.

Besides engaging in acquisitions, Roche used alliances and licensing deals to strengthen its presence in the field of cancer treatments. For instance, in 2007 Roche bought rights to an experimental vaccine program of a French biotech firm. Thus Roche had access to a therapeutic vaccine against cervical cancer and other diseases. Similarly, in 2010 Roche entered a deal with a US therapeutics firm to access their preclinical pipeline focusing on cancer and other diseases. The advantages of such partnership agreements are lower upfront costs and less risk compared to acquisitions, while they still offer access to innovative drugs. Specifically during the financial crisis, smaller drug developers became more willing to make deals in order to finance their research.

In light of the financial crisis Roche had to deal with an increase in pricing pressure for its highly priced cancer drugs, as austerity programs and healthcare reforms were introduced all over the world. Roche thus announced a restructuring program which included cutting 4,800 jobs over two years (approx. 6% of the company's overall staff) and transfers of 1,500 sales and internal jobs. In addition, Roche became more selective about its drugs in development. For example, the firm stopped investments in a diabetes drug, despite its well performance in studies. However, the potential benefits of the product were not far enough beyond a similar pill already sold. Compared with the industry, Roche's position during the financial crisis was still rather strong.

5.2.3 Almirall SA – initial public offering

One of the two companies in the sample that underwent an initial public offering during the investigation period is Almirall, SA. The company completed the IPO in June 2007, and issued a 30% stake in shares at the Madrid Stock Exchange. Almirall is based in Spain and is the country's 3rd largest pharmaceuticals company by market capitalization. As of December 31, 2008 the company was a 45.76%-owned affiliate of Grupo Plafin SA. Formerly called Laboratorios Almirall, SA it changed its name to Almirall, SA in July 2009. The company's leading therapeutic areas include its dermatology, cardiovascular, central nervous system, and respiratory divisions. Its products are made available in over 70 countries, either by the company's own marketing or through licensing. The firm's R&D expenditure as a percentage of sales started at 15.4% in 2007 and 2008, fell to 13.1% in 2009, and increased again to 16.4% of sales in 2010.

Reported results of Almirall during the investigation period

In 2007 Almirall successfully completed its IPO and achieved good results. Normalized net income increased by 15% while net income fell by 11%, partly due to extra charges linked to acquisitions. In total, net sales rose slightly with the international market being the growth driver. In the Spanish market sales rose only minimally. The Spanish market accounted for 66% of Almirall's total sales, demonstrating the high dependence on one country. R&D spending for pharmaceutical products rose by 40%, reflecting the firm's focus on progressing in its drug development. In 2007 Almirall acquired Hermal, a leading German dermatological company. Compared to the sample peer group, Almirall's performance measured in ROA was slightly below average. The current ratio was higher than in half of the sample firms.

In the year 2008 Almirall reported solid performance, with net income rising slightly. The strong growth in net sales was enabled through the integration of the newly acquired Hermal unit. Growth driver was the international market, with sales rising 35%. Almirall increased its R&D spending and number of employees. Its products Ebastine and Almotriptan achieved significant recovery since the first half of 2008. The ROA of the company improved compared to the peer group, and was above average. The current ratio was at the median.

Almirall sustained its performance in the year 2009, with net income rising 11% and sales growing slightly. The profit of the company was achieved mainly due to the sale of 13 non-strategic products from the portfolio in the first quarter. Sales growth was again driven by the international market. Almirall managed to expand more internationally and increased the share of international sales to 42% of the total sales compared to 34% in 2007. Besides the company experienced growth in its dermatological portfolio. R&D investments decreased as the company introduced costs containment measures. The ROA of Almirall was above average compared to the peer group. The current ratio was below average.

The company's performance in 2010 was weakened by overall economic pressures in the market, particularly within Spain, resulting in a decline of net profit. Total sales decreased, with the Spanish market accounting for a big share of the sales loss, mostly due to healthcare reforms imposed by the Spanish government. The company introduced further cost containment measures and increased R&D spending by 20%. The ROA and current ratio of the company were below average compared to the sample peer group, but remained above the median of the sample firms.

Strategy of Almirall and performance influencing aspects

Almirall develops proprietary drugs through its own R&D and markets licensed products from other pharmaceutical companies. The firm's products are diversified through multiple therapeutic areas. The gastrointestinal and dermatology divisions were in the focus because they were the key areas of growth. Through the acquisition of the prescription skincare business Hermal specialized further in dermatology. Besides, Almirall had a major technological platform for the development of inhalation products.

Almirall performed its IPO in June 2007 in order to gain access to domestic and international equity capital. The raised capital helped the company to further develop its existing drug pipeline, fund its R&D efforts for the next years and cover the company's costs associated with the launch of products. Besides, the IPO provided the company with a source of financing for acquisitions and licensing deals in order to expand more internationally.

Internationalization was one of the key objectives for Almirall. During the investigation period, the company had a very high dependence on the Spanish market. In 2007 for instance, approx. 66% of sales were achieved in Spain, 23% in Europe and the Middle East and only 9% of sales came from America, Africa or Asia. Following its IPO, Almirall made two major acquisitions in Europe in 2007, which contributed to its international expansion into key European markets. Almirall acquired the German company

Hermal and a portfolio of eight products from Shire. Both acquisitions strengthened the company's presence in Europe. In addition, Almirall opened new affiliates in Great Britain, Austria, Poland and Switzerland.

In the following years Almirall continued to selectively assess new business opportunities. Almirall focused on commercial agreements as well as intensifying the process of internationalization of its marketing activities and production processes. Specifically, Almirall developed several external partnerships and licensing agreements. Through license-out agreements Almirall was able to establish a presence in new markets. Besides, Almirall developed and marketed several drugs of major pharmaceutical companies through its own affiliates in Spain, and partly within Europe by license-in agreements. This was attractive for other firms due to the strong market position of Almirall in the Spanish market.

Like other pharmaceutical firms, Almirall faced patent expirations among its bestselling drugs. The top products of the firm include Ebastine, Atorvastatin, Escitalopram, and Plusvent. Out of the top ten products of the firm, the patents of four drugs expired in 2010. The entire top ten faced patent expiration and the threat of generic competition until 2014. The firm was trying to counter this threat by investing in R&D to develop a strong pipeline of new drugs, which includes products such as Eklira and the multiple sclerosis treatment Sativex. Sativex was developed in partnership with UK GW Pharmaceuticals plc and German Bayer AG, with Almirall holding the drug's marketing license in Spain and being GW's partner for the rest of Europe, except UK. The drug was the first prescription drug made from cannabis to officially go on sale anywhere in the world.

During the financial crisis, the firm's dependence on the Spanish and European market had a strongly negative impact on the firm. Especially in Europe, pharmaceutical companies rely heavily on state financed healthcare systems in order to generate revenue. When the financial crisis led to budget constraints among European governments, healthcare reforms and austerity programs were introduced. The Spanish government imposed a wide range of price cuts for patented drugs and encouraged the prescription of generic products instead of branded medicines. Smaller European based pharmaceutical firms like Almirall were hit hardest, resulting in falling revenues and lower performance. This highlighted the need for Almirall to widen its business to new products and new markets beyond Europe in order to generate sales growth. Besides, Almirall cut costs and became more selective in prioritizing projects to keep R&D costs down.

6 Discussion of the findings

The results of the quantitative and qualitative analysis for the four years under investigation offer valuable insights into the relationship between financial slack and corporate performance.

Overall the correlational analysis showed a significant positive correlation for current ratio and ROA_{ni} for all the years under investigation except 2009, where the correlation coefficient for the variables was not statistically significant. To be more exact, overall between 17% and 22% of the variance in ROA_{ni} could be explained by its relationship to current ratio in the examined years. Thus, the author of this thesis suggests that financial slack is positively related to corporate performance during crisis, which corresponds with findings of previous authors, such as Su *et al.* (2009) and Bradley *et al.* (2011a).. As expected, this leads to the rejection of the null hypothesis $H0_3$ stating that financial slack has no influence on corporate performance measured as ROA_{ni} during crisis.

For the other definitions of ROA however, the identified correlations were mostly negligible or statistically insignificant. Except in 2008, where $ROA_{pre\text{-}tax}$ showed a statistically significant moderate correlation with financial slack ($r=-397$ $p<.05$). The results on ROA_{EBITDA} did not reach significance at the 0.05 level in any year under investigation. This suggests that financial slack does not have a strong relationship with performance directly resulting from core operations during crisis. Hence the null hypotheses $H0_1$ and $H0_2$, stating that financial slack has no influence on corporate performance measured as ROA_{EBITDA} or $ROA_{pre\text{-}tax}$ during crisis, cannot be rejected.

Concerning the interpretation of the different results for the correlations of financial slack with the three performance metrics applied in this study, it has to be said that generally not enough consideration is given to the definition of measurement of performance in slack literature. Several authors use ROA as a performance metric, but do not state the exact definition applied (e.g. Latham and Braun, 2009; Chiu and Liaw, 2009; Greenley and Oktemgil, 1998). Thus it is difficult to interpret the results on the relationship between slack and performance in comparison to the findings of previous authors.

The fact that current ratio exhibits a strongly positive and significant correlation with ROA_{ni} in 2007, 2008 and 2010, but almost no correlation with the other ROA measures, indicates that financial slack particularly affects net income. The main difference to the other ROA measures is that the definition of net income includes extraordinary income of a firm, like restructuring charges, unusual or nonrecurring items and results from discontinued operations. Hence, one explanation for the link between financial slack and ROA_{ni} could be that slack minimizes a firm's need for restructuring, thus avoiding costly restructuring programs which affect the result form extraordinary items. In this regard, pharmaceutical firms seem to use financial slack resources as a buffer from negative influences of a threatening external environment.

Another interesting finding of this study concerns the correlation coefficients between the three ROA metrics themselves. As expected, the variables representing different definitions of ROA are generally highly correlated with each other ($r>.76$ $p<.01$ for all years except 2007). After all, each of them is based on a firm's earnings. In contrast to that, in 2007 ROA_{ni} does not show significant correlations with the other two performance measures, while ROA_{EBITDA} and $ROA_{pre\text{-}tax}$ are strongly correlated with each other. As mentioned above, the main difference between ROA_{ni} and the other measures of ROA is that the definition of net income also includes extraordinary P/L, such as income from discontinued operations. In the year 2007 several firms in the sample, including e.g. Novartis AG, Akzo Nobel NV, Bayer AG and Merck KGaA engaged in divestments of some form. Thus, they reported substantial income from discontinued operations resulting in a ROA_{ni} that differs significantly from the ROA_{EBITDA} or $ROA_{pre\text{-}tax}$.

These differences among the three performance metrics, as reported e.g. in the year 2007 bring up the topic of potential outliers. Outliers can have a harmful effect the statistical analysis, since the inclusion of an outlier can distort the correlation and regression results (cf. Wefald *et al.*, 2010a). The analysis to detect outliers showed one specific result, namely an extremely high ROA_{ni} of Akzo Nobel NV in 2007. Amounting to 48.49%, the value is approx. four standard deviations above the mean. This was caused by the firm's high extraordinary income from discontinued operations in that year. Another specific feature of the sample is the relatively high ROA values reported by Novo Nordisk A/S, with all three performance metrics lying around two standard deviations above the mean between 2008 and 2010. Concerning the current ratio, the firm Richter Gedeon Rt. could be regarded as an outlier since the firm's current ratio is more than 3.8 standard deviations from the mean in between 2007 and 2009. Besides, no further significant abnormalities were identified for the applied independent and dependent variables. In any case, it is important to note that the results of this analysis might possibly have been impacted to some extent by the presence of outliers.

Despite the above mentioned outlier in ROA_{ni} in 2007 as well as the lack of correlation between ROA_{ni} and the other ROA measures in this year, current ratio exhibits a significant correlation with the performance metric in this period. Similarly, in 2008 and 2010 current ratio has the strongest correlation with ROA_{ni}. Hence, during crisis financial slack resources seem to have a special link to the extraordinary income of a firm, irrespectively of the performance in core operations. One way to interpret this result as mentioned before is that financial slack affects net income by avoiding restructuring charges in the result form extraordinary items. Since correlational analysis solely provides evidence on the relationship between two variables, but not on the causal direction (cf. Bryman and Bell, 2011, p. 346) the causal influence could work in the other way. In this regard an explanation for the link between current ratio and ROA_{ni} in particular could be that non-recurring events influence the accumulation of financial slack during crisis. Hence, this study contributes to another aspect of slack literature, namely the research of conditions under which financial slack develops. Previous authors suggest that slack does not only influence performance, but the accumulation of slack resources itself is influenced by past performance. Authors argue that particularly in dynamic environments good performance leads to high levels of slack (cf. Sharfman *et al.*, 1988, p. 608; Voss *et al.*, 2008, p. 148). The results of the correlation analysis are an indicator for the fact that performance resulting from non-recurring events (e.g. discontinued operations) leads to higher levels of financial slack during a financial crisis. Since the divestment of business operations for instance can result in a profit, this can contribute to increased financial resources.

The findings from the qualitative analysis suggest that in addition to firm performance, the level of financial slack is the result of an intentional decision to maintain high levels of liquid financial resources. Novartis for example performed well and had high cash flows due to cancer drugs, but the firm chose to maintain rather low levels financial slack, indicated by a low current ratio, to improve efficiency.

Regarding the effect of the intervening variables on financial slack, basically no significant results were found through the correlational analysis. New products showed only weakly significant correlations with ROA_{EBITDA} ($r=.355$) and $ROA_{pre\text{-}tax}$ ($r=.374$) in the year 2007, but no significant correlation with ROA_{ni} at all. Besides, no correlations were identified for new products in any other years under investigation. Similarly, in 2007 a positive correlation was found for M&A activities and performance (ROA_{EBITDA} as well as $ROA_{pre-tax}$). This implies that M&A activity and performance could positively influence each other, however no such evidence was found for the other periods. The qualitative content analysis gives some closer insight into the possible link between financial slack and M&A activities. For instance, Roche Holding AG had a continuously high current ratio in the investigation period, implying high amounts of financial slack resources. The firm used its strong financial position to engage in acquisitions. The high level of financial slack allowed Roche maximum flexibility to exploit opportunities, which resulted in several acquisitions to strengthen the firm's position.

In order to make a statement on the effect of IPO, not enough data is available. As mentioned before, only two occurrences of IPO, for 2007 and 2010 were included in the sample. The correlation of IPO and M&A found in 2010 is not generalizable because it is only due to one firm. The result was generated as the firm Protek OAO undergoing an IPO in 2010 had a high number of M&A activities in the same year.

Consequently the propositions P_3 to P_5, stating that the factors new product approvals, M&A activities, and IPO influence the relationship between financial slack and performance during crisis, cannot be supported due to a lack of evidence.

The results from the qualitative research revealed that the financial crisis presented an environment characterized by low munificence, particularly regarding financial resources and high dynamism. One particular threat for the pharmaceutical industry was the price erosion, due to governments' austerity programs and changed consumer behavior. Besides, increased competition on the market (e.g. by generics) and a high level of environmental uncertainty posed further risks. As pointed out e.g. by Tan and Peng (2003, p. 1253) and Su *et al.* (2009, pp. 76–80) in such a dynamic environment, flexibility as well as strategic change and adaptation are a critical for a firm's survival and success. The financial crisis increased the firms' need for change of existing size and cost structures. Common reactions by pharmaceutical companies were the implementation of cost cutting and restructuring measures, including job cuts and focus on efficiency and productivity. However, slack can act as a buffer in this regard. If excess financial resources are available to a firm, it can maintain strategic investments and initially avoid staff reductions despite a possible decrease in revenues (cf. Latham and Braun, 2009, pp. 34–35). Roche Holding AG, for example continued to engage in M&A investments throughout the investigation period. The firm first officially introduced cost-cutting measures due to the financial crisis in September 2010 when its situation was still comparatively well, while other firms had to start cutting jobs already in the first years of the financial crisis. This result could help explain why the quantitative analysis showed a significant correlation between financial slack and performance measured as ROA_{ni}.

The crisis also affected the M&A market through increasing uncertainty and diminishing valuations of companies. Since the financial markets were weakened, it became harder for firms to access financial resources externally. In this regard, a high level of financial slack can enable a firm to actively engage in acquisitions, despite a turbulent and uncertain external environment such as the financial crisis (cf. Iyer and Miller, 2008). In addition, financial slack shields a firm from external risk and uncertainty to some extent, allowing firms to engage in more investment activities in the face of high uncertainty (cf. Zona, 2012, p. 44). This corresponds with the function of slack as a facilitator of strategic behavior in the literature. While firms with low liquidity might hesitate to make acquisitions due to financing problems, firms with sufficient financial resources can use the high uncertainty in markets to their advantage. Roche's strong, specialized drug portfolio for instance was achieved through heavy investments in M&A. Acquisitions can lead to synergies and long-term cost improvements while in the short term they result in integration and restructuring costs, thus influencing performance in two ways.

Su *et al.* (2009, pp. 76–80) point out that in dynamic and resource scarce environments it is essential for firms to develop new opportunities internally, e.g. through the introduction of new products, in order to sustain their competitive advantages and enhance performance. The newspaper research showed that acquisitions can be one way for a pharmaceutical firm to extend and strengthen their drug pipeline under development, leading to an increased number of product introductions in the long term. Novartis engaged in high investments in R&D and additionally diversified through acquisitions. Thereby the firm was able to generate one of the richest drug portfolios in the industry.

The sample did not include enough evidence on firms undergoing an IPO during crisis to make a statement on the intervening effect of the variable on the relationship between slack and performance. Due to the unpredictability during the period of an IPO a firm's financial resources generally become scarcer and thus more valuable. The uncertainty and low munificence of the financial crisis additionally increase this effect. In the case of Almirall, SA a relatively high current ratio of 3.13 was reported in the year before the IPO. This may have contributed to the success of the IPO in 2007, where the current ratio of the firm was still higher than in 50% of the sample firms (1.64). The main reason for Almirall to undergo the IPO was access to a new source of financing. Thus the firm was able to engage in M&A activities to strengthen its portfolio and expand internationally.

In summary the author found that financial slack influences corporate performance measured as ROA_{ni} during crisis ($H0_1$), while the effect on $ROA_{pre\text{-}tax}$ and ROA_{EBITDA} could not be supported ($H0_2$ and $H0_3$). The correlational analysis did not provide enough evidence to confirm the propositions P_1 to P_3. However, the qualitative content analysis implied that new product introductions and M&A activities are enabled by high levels of slack and lead to a strong portfolio and increased performance during crisis.

7 Conclusion and forecast

This thesis examines the relationship between financial slack and performance during the financial crisis between 2007 and 2010, taking into account three intervening factors. The empirical analysis of the sample of 25 European pharmaceutical firms includes correlational and regression analysis of financial data as well as qualitative content analysis of newspaper articles.

Literature that is concerned with slack comprises two main perspectives on its effects. Resource based and behavioral theorists stress the active role of managers and argue that organizational slack allows a firm room to use excess resources to enhance performance. Agency theory on the other hand puts an emphasis on the opportunistic behavior of managers, according to which slack creates inefficiencies which result in a negative effect on firm performance. When adding the uncertain and resource scarce environment of a financial crisis to the consideration, authors argue that financial slack becomes increasingly beneficial for a firm. The findings of this study contribute to the understanding of the role that financial slack plays during crisis.

The results provide some evidence of a positive relationship between unabsorbed, financial slack and corporate performance during crisis. Specifically the research showed that financial slack measured as current ratio is positively related to performance measured as ROA_{ni} ($H0_1$). Consistent with the resource based view and behavioral theory of the firm, this result suggests that firms use slack to buffer their operations from a turbulent external environment and improve performance. However, regarding the correlation of financial slack with the other two measures of corporate performance, ROA_{EBITDA} and $ROA_{pre\text{-}tax}$ ($H0_2$ and $H0_3$), the empirical analysis showed no significant results.

The findings of the correlational research can be additionally used to shed some light on the conditions under which financial slack is accumulated. The fact that current ratio correlates with ROA_{ni}, despite the lack of correlations with other ROA measures, indicates that good performance allows the development of higher amounts of financial slack resources. During a financial crisis, especially profits from non-recurring events such as the divestment of business operations seem to contribute to increased slack resources.

While the correlational analysis does not provide enough evidence on the effect of the intervening variables M&A, IPO and new products in order to confirm the propositions P_3 to P_5, the qualitative content analysis delivers insight into their relationship with financial slack and performance. Especially new product developments and M&A activities are facilitated by high levels of slack. Due to weak financial markets, financial slack resources enable a firm to engage in investments in product innovation as well as M&A. Both of these activities help generate a strong portfolio of drugs and which can lead to increased performance during crisis.

Furthermore, the author of this thesis offers a possible explanation for the conflicting results of previous research on the relationship, by pointing out the critical role of measurement of slack as well as performance. The three slightly different definitions of the performance measure ROA used in this thesis resulted in widely differing results. In previous research, authors frequently fail to adequately specify the exact definitions used for the applied variables. This can make it difficult to compare the findings of different studies.

In summary, this thesis confirms that financial slack is linked to corporate performance. While the findings provide some evidence for the arguments of resource based view and behavioral theory, the perspective of agency theorists is not supported in the light of a crisis. Hence, the author of this thesis argues for a positive relationship between slack and performance. One side of this relationship is that slack influences performance. However, on the other hand, the accumulation of financial slack can also be influenced by corporate performance.

7.1 Limitations of the study

This thesis has several limitations which offer room for further research. These aspects are discussed in these final sections of this thesis. First, only a small sample of firms (25) was used to test the propositions in this study. All of these firms are large companies, identified through high operating revenue. For instance, none of the sample firms had less than 1000 employees in any year during the entire sample period[10]. Furthermore all of the sample firms operate in the same industry (pharmaceuticals) and are locat-

---

[10] For three firms (Actelion ltd., Farmacol SA, Pelion SA) no information was provided on the number of employees for some of the years.

ed in the same region (Eastern and Western Europe). The small number of sample firms however, resulted in limited generalizability of the results. Despite the restriction of the sample to one single industry in order to generate a homogenous sample and prevent biased results, the firms in the sample naturally exhibit some differences. All the firms were identified by a NACE Rev. 2 core code 212 as manufacturers of pharmaceutical preparations. While some firms are more diversified in their operations (e.g. Bayer AG) others have a very narrow focus on pharmaceuticals (e.g. Roche Holding AG).

Moreover, this thesis examines solely financial slack, which is one specific type of organizational slack among several other categories. However, prior studies provide evidence on the fact that different slack types, such as absorbed or potential slack influence an organization differently (cf. Mishina *et al.*, 2004, p. 1191; Sigerstad, 2004, p. 44). In addition, various measures can be applied for slack. The author of this study chose to apply current ratio as one single measure for financial slack. Besides for performance, ROA is chosen as a measure, with three different definitions being used. The use of different or multiple measures for both performance and slack could produce different results.

Since prior studies suggest that intervening variables exist for the relationship of slack and performance (cf. Daniel *et al.*, 2004, p. 572), the author of this thesis investigates the influence of three specific factors on the dependent and independent variables. However, additional moderating variables might exist. Besides, the limited amount of data led to the fact that the propositions concerning new products, M&A and IPO could not be supported.

Concerning the qualitative content analysis of newspaper articles the investigation is limited to three major international business newspapers. This excludes e.g. smaller and more regional newspapers, which might provide a different perspective.

7.2 Potential for future research

The above mentioned limitations of this thesis suggest further investigation of several aspects. First, future efforts should extend similar inquiries to international and other industrial settings to compare the applicability of various theories in different cultural and institutional backgrounds. Besides, larger and more diverse samples, e.g. in terms of firm size and age could enhance the generalizability of future empirical testing.

Second, since different slack types, such unabsorbed, absorbed or potential slack have shown to influence an organization differently (cf. Mishina *et al.*, 2004, p. 1191; Sigerstad, 2004, p. 44), future investigation of the effect of other forms of slack on performance, specifically under threatening environmental conditions could provide additional valuable insight in the concept of slack.

The propositions concerning the intervening variables in this study could not be supported due to a lack of evidence. A larger sample with more extensive data on new products, M&A and IPO could lead to stronger results. In addition, next to the intervening variables employed in this study, other factors might influence the way slack affects performance. Hence, future research may extend this analysis to capture the impact of other intervening variables on the slack-performance link.

An additional direction for future research could be the examination of the impact of different ways of measurement for slack as well as performance. The results on the three ROA measures employed in this study indicate that the choice of measures has a critical effect on the results.

8 List of references

a) Books, collected editions and dissertations

Berg, B.L. (2001) *Qualitative research methods for the social sciences,* 4th ed., Allyn and Bacon, Boston.

Bryman, A. and Bell, E. (2011) *Business research methods,* 3rd ed., Oxford University Press, Cambridge, New York.

Carton, R.B. and Hofer, C.W. (2007) *Measuring organizational performance: Metrics for entrepreneurship and strategic management research*, Edward Elgar, Cheltenham.

Creswell, J.W. (2003) *Research design: Qualitative, quantitative, and mixed method approaches,* 2nd ed., Sage Publications, Thousand Oaks, Calif.

Cyert, R.M. and March, J.G. (1963) *A behavioral theory of the firm*, Prentice-Hall, Englewood Cliffs, NJ.

Krause, H.-U. and Arora, D. (2010) *Controlling-Kennzahlen, Key Performance Indicators: Zweisprachiges Handbuch Deutsch/Englisch,* 2nd ed., Oldenbourg, München.

Losbichler, H., Hofer, P., Eisl, C. and Zauner, B. (2012) "An Investigation of ROCE and Its Drivers: Empirical Analysis of European Companies", in Jodlbauer, H., Olhager, J. and Schonberger, R.J. (Eds.), *Modelling Value, Contributions to Management Science*, Physica-Verlag HD, pp. 119-148.

March, J.G. and Simon, H.A. (1958) *Organizations*, Wiley, New York.

Mayring, P. (2010) *Qualitative Inhaltsanalyse: Grundlagen und Techniken, Beltz Pädagogik,* 11th ed., Beltz, Weinheim.

Mousa, F.-T. (2009) "When do Slack Resources impact new venture success?", Dissertation, College of Business, Washington State University, 2009.

Penrose, E.T. (1959) *The theory of the growth of the firm*, Oxford University Press, Oxford, New York.

Rasch, B. (2010) *Quantitative Methoden: Band 1: Einführung in die Statistik für Psychologen und Sozialwissenschaftler, Springer-Lehrbuch,* 3rd ed., Springer, Berlin.

Scharfenkamp, N. (1987) *Organisatorische Gestaltung und wirtschaftlicher Erfolg: Organizational slack als Ergebnis und Einflußfaktor der formalen Organisationsstruktur*, De Gruyter, Berlin u.a.

Sigerstad, T.D. (2004) "To what extent is slack conditioned on munificence? Extending the behavioral theory of the firm", Dissertation, College of Business, University of Oklahoma, Norman, Oklahoma, 2004.

Venanzi, D. (2012) "Criticism of the Accounting-Based Measures of Performance", in Venanzi, D. (Ed.), *Financial Performance Measures and Value Creation: the State of the Art*, Springer Milan, Milano, pp. 1–8.

Weidermann, P.H. (1984) *Das Management des Organizational Slack*, Gabler, Wiesbaden.

b) Journal articles and working papers

Adjei, F. (2012) "Debt dependence and corporate performance in a financial crisis: evidence from the sub-prime mortgage crisis", *Journal of Economics and Finance*, Vol. 36 No. 1, pp. 176–189, DOI: 10.1007/s12197-010-9140-0.

Baum, C.F., Caglayan, M.O., Ozkan, N. and Talavera, O. (2004) "The Impact of Macroeconomic Uncertainty on Cash Holdings for Non-Financial Firms", *SSRN Electronic Journal*, DOI: 10.2139/ssrn.555952.

Bourgeois III, L.J. and Singh, J.V. (1983) "Organizational Slack and Political Behavior Among Top Management Teams", *Academy of Management Proceedings,* August 1983, pp. 43–47, DOI: 10.5465/AMBPP.1983.4976315.

Bourgeois, L.J. (1981) "On the Measurement of Organizational Slack", *Academy of Management Review*, Vol. 6 No. 1, pp. 29–39, DOI: 10.5465/AMR.1981.4287985.

Bradley, S.W., Shepherd, D.A. and Wiklund, J. (2011a) "The Importance of Slack for New Organizations Facing 'Tough' Environments", *Journal of Management Studies*, Vol. 48 No. 5, pp. 1071–1097, DOI: 10.1111/j.1467-6486.2009.00906.x.

Bradley, S.W., Wiklund, J. and Shepherd, D.A. (2011b) "Swinging a double-edged sword: The effect of slack on entrepreneurial management and growth", *Journal of Business Venturing*, Vol. 26 No. 5, pp. 537–554, DOI: 10.1016/j.jbusvent.2010.03.002.

Brunnermeier, M.K. (2008) “Deciphering the 2007-08 Liquidity and Credit Crunch”, *National Bureau of Economic Research Working Paper Series*, Working Paper 14612.

Campello, M., Graham, J. and Harvey, C.R. (2009) “The Real Effects of Financial Constraints: Evidence from a Financial Crisis”, *National Bureau of Economic Research Working Paper Series,* Working Paper 15552.

Castrogiovanni, G.J. (1991) “Environmental Munificence: A Theoretical Assessment”, *Academy of Management Review*, Vol. 16 No. 3, pp. 542–565.

Cheng, J.L.C. and Kesner, I.F. (1997) “Organizational Slack and Response to Environmental Shifts: The Impact of Resource Allocation Patterns”, *Journal of Management*, Vol. 23 No. 1, pp. 1–18, DOI: 10.1177/014920639702300101

Chiu, Y.-C. and Liaw, Y.-C. (2009) “Organizational slack: is more or less better?”, *Journal of Organizational Change Management*, Vol. 22 No. 3, pp. 321–342, DOI: 10.1108/09534810910951104.

Daniel, F., Lohrke, F.T., Fornaciari, C.J. and Turner, R. (2004) “Slack resources and firm performance: a meta-analysis”, *Journal of Business Research*, Vol. 57 No. 6, pp. 565–574, DOI: 10.1016/S0148-2963(02)00439-3.

Duncan, R.B. (1972) “Characteristics of Organizational Environments and Perceived Environmental Uncertainty”, *Administrative Science Quarterly*, Vol. 17 No. 3, pp. 313–327.

Dunk, A.S. and Nouri, H. (1998) “Antecedents of budgetary slack: A literature review and synthesis”, *Journal of Accounting Literature*, Vol. 17, pp. 72–96.

Duriau, V.J., Reger, R.K. and Pfarrer, M.D. (2007) “A Content Analysis of the Content Analysis Literature in Organization Studies: Research Themes, Data Sources, and Methodological Refinements”, *Organizational Research Methods*, Vol. 10 No. 1, pp. 5–34, DOI: 10.1177/1094428106289252.

Edmondson, A.C. and McManus, S.E. (2007) “Methodological Fit in Management Field Research”, *Academy of Management Review*, Vol. 32 No. 4, pp. 1155–1179, DOI: 10.5465/AMR.2007.26586086.

Elmassri, M. and Harris, E. (2011) "Rethinking budgetary slack as budget risk management", *Journal of Applied Accounting Research*, Vol. 12 No. 3, pp. 278–293, DOI: 10.1108/09675421111187700.

George, G. (2005) "Slack Resources and the Performance of Privately Held Firms", *Academy of Management Journal*, Vol. 48 No. 4, pp. 661–676, DOI: 10.5465/AMJ.2005.17843944

Greenley, G.E. and Oktemgil, M. (1998) "A Comparison of Slack Resources in High and Low Performing British Companies", *Journal of Management Studies*, Vol. 35 No. 3, pp. 377–398, DOI: 10.1111/1467-6486.00098.

Han, S. and Qiu, J. (2007) "Corporate precautionary cash holdings", *Journal of Corporate Finance*, Vol. 13 No. 1, pp. 43–57, DOI: 10.1016/j.jcorpfin.2006.05.002.

Harris, H. (2001) "Content Analysis of Secondary Data: A Study of Courage in Managerial Decision Making", *Journal of Business Ethics*, Vol. 34 3/4, pp. 191–208, DOI: 10.1023/A:1012534014727.

Heng, L. and Xiuhao, D. (2010) "Organizational Slack, Entrepreneurial Orientation and Product Innovativeness: Evidence from China", *Academy of Management Annual Meeting Proceedings*, Vol. 8 No. 1, pp. 1–7, DOI: 10.5465/ AMBPP.2010.54498610.

Herold, D.M., Jayaraman, N. and Narayanaswamy, C.R. (2006) "What is the Relationship between Organizational Slack and Innovation?", *Journal of Managerial Issues*, Vol. 18 No. 3, pp. 372–392.

Iyer, D.N. and Miller, K.D. (2008) "Performance Feedback, Slack and the Timing of Acquisitions", *Academy of Management Journal*, Vol. 51 No. 4, pp. 808–822, DOI: 10.5465/AMR.2008.33666024

Johansson, A.C. (2011) "Financial Markets in East Asia and Europe during the Global Financial Crisis", *The World Economy*, Vol. 34 No. 7, pp. 1088–1105, DOI: 10.1111/j.1467-9701.2011.01366.x.

Ju, M. and Zhao, H. (2009) "Behind organizational slack and firm performance in China: The moderating roles of ownership and competitive intensity", *Asia Pacific Journal of Management*, Vol. 26 No. 4, pp. 701–717, DOI: 10.1007/s10490-009-9148-1.

Katila, R. and Shane, S. (2005) "When Does Lack of Resources Make New Firms Innovative?", *Academy of Management Journal*, Vol. 48 No. 5, pp. 814–829, DOI: 10.5465/AMJ.2005.18803924

Koberg, C.S. (1987) "Resource Scarcity, Environmental Uncertainty, and Adaptive Organizational Behavior", *Academy of Management Journal*, Vol. 30 No. 4, pp. 798–807, DOI: 10.2307/256161.

Krcal, H.-C. (2012) "Eine neue konzeptionelle Perspektive auf Arten des Organizational Slack", *Zeitschrift für betriebswirtschaftliche Forschung*, Vol. 64, pp. 679–717.

Latham, S.F. and Braun, M.R. (2009) "Assessing the Relationship between Financial Slack and Company Performance during an Economic Recession: An Empirical Study", *International Journal of Management*, Vol. 26 No. 1, pp. 33–39.

Lawson, M.B. (2001) "In praise of slack: Time is of the essence", *Academy of Management Executive*, Vol. 15 No. 3, pp. 125–135, DOI: 10.5465/AME.2001.5229658.

Lee, S. (2011) "How Financial Slack Affects Firm Performance: Evidence from US Industrial Firms", *Journal of Economic Research*, Vol. 16, pp. 1–27.

Lin, W.-T., Cheng, K.-Y. and Liu, Y. (2009) "Organizational slack and firm's internationalization: A longitudinal study of high-technology firms", *Journal of World Business*, Vol. 44 No. 4, pp. 397–406, DOI: 10.1016/j.jwb.2008.11.003.

Love, G.E. and Nohria, N. (2005) "Reducing slack: the performance consequences of downsizing by large industrial firms, 1977-93", *Strategic Management Journal*, Vol. 26 No. 12, pp. 1087–1108, DOI: 10.1002/smj.487.

Majumdar, S.K. (1998) "Slack in the state-owned enterprise: An evaluation of the impact of soft-budget constraints", *International Journal of Industrial Organization*, Vol. 16, pp. 337–394, DOI: 10.1016/S0167-7187(96)01043-0.

Marino, K.E. and Lange, D.R. (1983) "Measuring Organizational Slack: A Note on the Convergence and Divergence of Alternative Operational Definitions", *Journal of Management*, Vol. 9 No. 1, pp. 81–92, DOI: 10.1177/014920638300900108

Martinez, R.J. and Kendall, A. (2006) "An Examination of Firm Slack and Risk-Taking in Regulated and Deregulated Airlines", *Journal of Managerial Issues*, Vol. 18 No. 1, pp. 11–31.

McMullen, J.S. and Shepherd, D.A. (2006) "Entrepreneurial Action and the Role of Uncertainty in the Theory of the Entrepreneur", *Academy of Management Review*, Vol. 31 No. 1, pp. 132–152, DOI: 10.5465/AMR.2006.19379628.

Mellahi, K. and Wilkinson, A. (2010) "A Study of the Association between Level of Slack Reduction Following Downsizing and Innovation Output", *Journal of Management Studies*, Vol. 47 No. 3, pp. 483–508, DOI: 10.1111/j.1467-6486.2009.00872.x.

Milliken, F.J. (1987) "Three types of perceived uncertainty about the environment: state, effect, and response uncertainty.", *Academy of Management Review*, Vol. 12 No. 1, pp. 133–143.

Mishina, Y., Pollock, T.G. and Porac, J.F. (2004) "Are more resources always better for growth? Resource stickiness in market and product expansion", *Strategic Management Journal*, Vol. 25 No. 12, pp. 1179–1197, DOI: 10.1002/smj.424.

Modi, S.B. and Mishra, S. (2011) "What drives financial performance–resource efficiency or resource slack?", *Journal of Operations Management*, Vol. 29 No. 3, pp. 254–273, DOI: 10.1016/j.jom.2011.01.002.

Moses, O.D. (1992) "Organizational slack and risk-taking behaviour: Tests of product pricing strategy", *Journal of Organizational Change Management*, Vol. 5 No. 3, pp. 38–54, DOI: 10.1108/09534819210018045.

Mousa, F.-T. and Reed, R. (2013) "The Impact of Slack Resources on High-Tech IPOs", *Entrepreneurship Theory and Practice*, DOI: 10.1111/etap.12001.

Nohria, N. and Gulati, R. (1996) "Is Slack Good or Bad for Innovation?", *Academy of Management Journal*, Vol. 39 No. 5, pp. 1245–1264, DOI: 10.2307/256998.

Nohria, N. and Gulati, R. (1997) "What is the Optimum Amount of Organizational Slack? A Study of the Relationship between Slack and Innovation of Multinational Firms", *European Management Journal*, Vol. 15 No. 6, pp. 603–611, DOI: 10.1016/S0263-2373(97)00044-3.

Opler, T., Pinkowitz, L., Stulz, R. and Williamson Rohan (1999) "The determinants and implications of corporate cash holdings", *Journal of*

Financial Economics, Vol. 52 No. 1, pp. 3–46, DOI: 10.1016/S0304-405X(99)00003-3.

Pál, R. and Ferrando, A. (2010) "Financing constraints and firms' cash policy in the euro area", *The European Journal of Finance*, Vol. 16 No. 2, pp. 153–171, DOI: 10.1080/13518470903075748.

Patzelt, H., Shepherd, D.A., Deeds, D. and Bradley, S.W. (2008) "Financial slack and venture managers' decisions to seek a new alliance", *Journal of Business Venturing*, Vol. 23 No. 4, pp. 465–481, DOI: 10.1016/j.jbusvent.2007.06.001.

Ramezani, C.A. (2011) "Financial constraints, real options and corporate cash holdings", *Managerial Finance*, Vol. 37 No. 12, pp. 1137–1160, DOI: 10.1108/ 03074351111175074.

Ramírez, A. and Tadesse, S. (2009) "Corporate cash holdings, uncertainty avoidance, and the multinationality of firms", *International Business Review*, Vol. 18 No. 4, pp. 387–403, DOI: 10.1016/j.ibusrev.2009.02.013.

Sharfman, M.P., Wolf, G., Chase, R.B. and Tansik, D.A. (1988) "Antecedents of Organizational Slack", *Academy of Management Review*, Vol. 13 No. 4, pp. 601–614.

Singh, J.V. (1986) "Performance, Slack, and Risk Taking in Organizational Decision Making", *Academy of Management Journal*, Vol. 29 No. 3, pp. 562–585.

Su, Z., Xie, E. and Li, Y. (2009) "Organizational slack and firm performance during institutional transitions", *Asia Pacific Journal of Management*, Vol. 26 No. 1, pp. 75–91, DOI: 10.1007/s10490-008-9101-8.

Tan, J. (2003) "Curvilinear Relationship Between Organizational Slack and Firm Performance", *European Management Journal*, Vol. 21 No. 6, pp. 740–749, DOI: 10.1016/j.emj.2003.09.010.

Tan, J. and Peng, M.W. (2003) "Organizational slack and firm performance during economic transitions: two studies from an emerging economy", *Strategic Management Journal*, Vol. 24 No. 13, pp. 1249–1263, DOI: 10.1002/smj.351.

Vanacker, T., Collewaert, V. and Paeleman, I. (2013) "The Relationship between Slack Resources and the Performance of Entrepreneurial Firms: The Role of Venture Capital and Angel Investors", *Journal of Management Studies*, pp. n/a, DOI: 10.1111/joms.12026.

Voss, G.B., Sirdeshmukh, D. and Voss, Z.G. (2008) "The Effects of Slack Resources and Environmental Threat on Product Exploration and Exploitation", *Academy of Management Journal*, Vol. 51 No. 1, pp. 147–164, DOI: 10.5465/AMJ.2008.30767373.

Wan, W.P. and Yiu, D.W. (2009) "From crisis to opportunity: environmental jolt, corporate acquisitions, and firm performance", *Strategic Management Journal*, Vol. 30 No. 7, pp. 791–801, DOI: 10.1002/smj.744.

Wefald, A.J., Katz, J.P., Downey, R.G. and Rust, K.G. (2010a) "Organizational Slack And Performance: The Impact Of Outliers", *The Journal of Applied Business Research*, Vol. 26 No. 1.

Wefald, A.J., Katz, J.P., Downey, R.G. and Rust, K.G. (2010b) "Organizational Slack, Firm Performance, and the Role of Industry", *Journal of Managerial Issues*, Vol. 22 No. 1, pp. 70–87.

Zona, F. (2012) "Corporate Investing as a Response to Economic Downturn: Prospect Theory, the Behavioural Agency Model and the Role of Financial Slack", *British Journal of Management*, Vol. 23, pp. 42–57, DOI: 10.1111/j.1467-8551.2012.00818.x.

c) Other sources

European Commission (2011) *Overview of the EU's pharmaceuticals sector*, available at: http://trade.ec.europa.eu/doclib/docs/2012/january/tradoc_148988.pdf (accessed 1 April 2013).

European Medicines Agency (2009) *New visual identity, web/e-mail addresses and organisation chart of the European Medicines Agency*, available at: http://www.epha.org/ IMG/pdf/EMEA_Communication_NewVisiualIdentity_en.pdf (accessed 23 March 2013)

Kelley, T. (2009) "Merck Takeover Fuels Speculation of Drugmaker Mergers", *Bloomberg News,* 9 March 2009, available at: http://www.bloomberg.com/apps/news?pid=newsarchive&sid=aoLqqDCxJJjg&refer=home (accessed 23 March 2013).

PharmaWatch (2008) "Opportunity knocks for big pharmaceutical companies in the credit crunch", *PharmaWatch: Biotechnology*, Vol. 7 No. 11, pp. 19–21.

MIX
Papier aus verantwortungsvollen Quellen
Paper from responsible sources
FSC® C105338

If you have any concerns about our products,
you can contact us on
ProductSafety@springernature.com

In case Publisher is established outside the EU,
the EU authorized representative is:
Springer Nature Customer Service Center GmbH
Europaplatz 3, 69115 Heidelberg, Germany

Printed by Libri Plureos GmbH
in Hamburg, Germany